No,
We Are Not Playing Dodge Ball

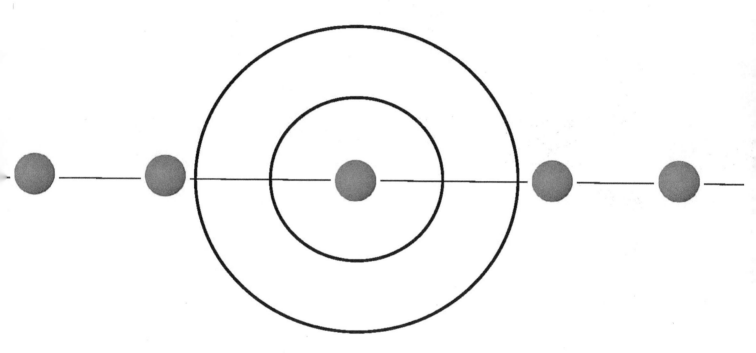

Elementary Physical Education
Games and Activities

Mike Bohannon

No, We Are Not Playing Dodge Ball

Author: Mike Bohannon

Front cover art: Randall E. Johnson
Interior Design: Leo Ward, Randall E. Johnson, Mike Bohannon

published by:
Five Stones Publishing
a division of:
The International Localization Network
ILNcenter.com
email: info@ilncenter.com

Dedication

GOD HAS BLESSED ME WITH A WONDERFUL FAMILY. I dedicate this book to them. To my beautiful wife Annette, my best friend and love of my life, Thank you for all your love and support. To my sons, Nolan and Luke, I am very proud of you. I cannot imagine what my life would be like without all of you.

Table of Contents

Chapter 4

Extras

Acknowledgements

I WANT TO THANK GOD FOR THE OPPORTUNITY TO TEACH and to share these ideas with other physical education teachers. I would also like to thank:

- My wife and sons, for their daily love, support and inspiration.
- My parents, for sending me to college.
- KAHPERD, Kansas Association of Health, Physical Education, Recreation and Dance, for promoting physical education and supporting physical education teachers throughout the state.
- Artie Kamiya and everyone involved with the _Great Activities Newspaper_
- Human Kinetics, for the many resources they provide for teachers.
- The many outstanding teachers, staff members and students that I have had the privilege to work with over the years.
- My school sister, Connie, for the notebook to write many games and ideas in.
- My high school English teacher Mrs. Bach for not putting up with my whining about work and pushing me to work harder.
- My high school College Prep English teacher Miss Scott, and the amazing Kelly Smith for proofreading this book.
- My high school Physical Education teacher and coach Ted Jantz for believing in me and inspiring me to be a teacher.
- The kids whose pictures I took for the book and their families for allowing me to use those pictures.
- Ms. Aeschilman, elementary Art Teacher, for her help with the Color Wheel Game.
- Mr. Nichol, Music teacher, for his help with music and lighting.
- Mrs. O., for getting me started out the right way at the beginning of my career by guiding me through student teaching.
- Mrs. Moyers for her help and advice in the writing of this book.
- Randy Johnson for all his help in publishing this book.
- Special Thanks to my colleague Greg Miller, middle school physical education teacher, for his support, guidance, and friendship for more than twenty years.

Introduction

In the 25 years I have taught elementary physical education I have not played a game of dodge ball. But every now and then, when one of my classes is walking into the gym, one of my students will say, "Are we playing dodge ball?" My answer is always the same:

"No, we are not playing dodge ball." I believe there are other games and activities involving teamwork and competition that will help improve eye-hand coordination, throwing, dodging, and catching without throwing a ball at someone else. This book is a collection of those games and activities. During my teaching career I have made an effort to learn from others and to try and keep my approach to teaching elementary physical education fun and fresh by trying new games and activities. I have attended many physical education workshops and conferences. I have read numerous books and gone to observe others teach.

All of these resources helped me to stay focused and motivated me to create some games of my own to keep the kids in class active and excited about physical activity. I believe this book can be a resource for other elementary physical education teachers to supplement what you are already doing in your classrooms.

Chapter One: Warm-ups

The first five minutes of class gets students going physically and mentally. The warm-up will vary depending on what the activity is for that day. Using different warm-up activities keeps the beginning of class exciting because the kids don't know what the warm-up will be today. I have warm-ups using equipment and others involving just movement and exercises. I have used all of the warm-ups and they are accompanied by a picture or drawings when needed. Some of the warm-ups lead right into the main activity by using the same equipment as the main activity.

Chapter Two: Integrated Games and Activities

This chapter has games that integrate math, spelling, music and art with physical activity. The kids are doing math and spelling while they are moving, throwing, rolling, kicking, and catching. I ask the teachers for their weekly newsletter and spelling list to keep me up to date on what is happening in each grade level. Integration is certainly not the sole purpose of physical education, but I do believe it is part of physical education and a student's well-rounded education. There are 26 integrated games and activities that can be used throughout the year. We will be reinforcing math and spelling skills with activities using basketball, football, bowling, hula hoops, foam dice, stompers and more. Kids love to show what they know and integration is a great way for them to do that. There are over 50 pictures and drawings to go along with detailed instructions for each activity.

Chapter Three: Games, Lead up Games, and Station Activities

This chapter is about individual skill development, teamwork, competition and cooperation. The games and activities in this chapter are designed to keep kids moving and thinking while working with others. There are 32 easy-to- use games and activities in this chapter. All are accompanied by detailed instructions, along with pictures and drawings. There is one station activity to be used at Halloween. All of the games and activities in this chapter can be modified to fit your needs.

Chapter Four: Reproducible Pictures and Handouts

Many of the games need a worksheet, or pictures, to be laminated. This chapter has the worksheets and pictures you need.

There are no dodge ball games in this book but there are a lot of fun, easy-to-use games, lead up games, station activities, and integrated activities that involve throwing, catching, dodging, strategy, teamwork and cooperation that will get your kids thinking and moving. There are pictures and illustrations to go with the warm-ups, games, lead-up games, and integrated activities that your kids will love. There are tips to help with class set up and organization. The pages in the reproducible chapter are to be copied and used with games and activities in this book. From warm-ups to reproducible pages and everything in between, this book will be a great resource to be used throughout the year and for years to come.

Chapter 1

Warm-Ups

A B C Warm – Up

K-5

Equipment needed: six cones.

Using the cones divide the gym into three areas and split the class up into three groups. Place one group in each area: A, B, and C. The students in each group will perform an exercise for 20 seconds and then rotate to the next area: A to B, B to C, and C to A. The students will do the exercise in each area to complete one round. We usually do two rounds. We use music to signal when the exercise starts and stops.

Example:

Round 1 – Area A, outside the cones, Jog; Area B, push-ups; Area C, Ski Jumps

Students will perform the exercise in their area for 20 seconds, then stop the music and have them rotate to the next area, then start the music again. When students are back where they started the round is over. Explain the exercises for the next round.

Round 2 - Area A, Gallop; Area B, Jumping Jacks; Area C, Crab push-ups

After two rounds, have the class walk for 30 seconds around the cones. Many exercises can be used with this warm-up. You could also use jump ropes.

We use the ABC warm-up in our basketball unit.

Round 1: The students dribble clockwise with the left hand in area A, Bounce pass in area B, Chest Pass in area C.

Round 2: Dribble counter-clockwise with the right hand in area A, overhead pass in area B, and push pass in area C. Ball handling skills could also be used, like figure eights.

Tips

We like to use music to signal the start and stop of the exercise, but a whistle could be used. You can put a sleeve on the cones with a letter in the pocket to show what area they are in (see the picture).Students should always be moving in the same direction in Area A.

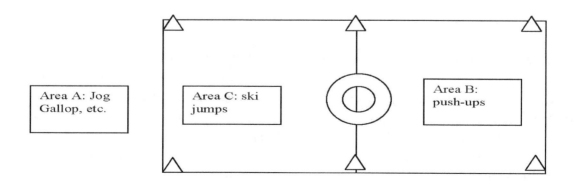

Bean Bag warm-up

K-3

Equipment needed: Bean Bags (one for each person)

Each student will have a bean bag. When the music is playing or on your command, students will travel with the bean bag (skip, gallop, slide step, walk, walk backwards, seal walk, crab walk). When the music stops or on your command they will stop and perform the exercise you call out. You decide how many they will do.

- Skip while holding on to the bean bag
- Seal walk with the bean bag on their back
- Three push-ups with the bean bag on their back
- Walk with the bean bag on their head
- Crab walk with the bean bag on their stomach or chest
- Four crab push-ups with the bean bag on their stomach
- Gallop while holding on to the bean bag
- Toss the bean bag above their head and catch it (five times)
- Walk backwards with the bean bag on their shoulder, looking over the shoulder with the bean bag on it.
- Ten ski jumps over the bean bag on the floor
- Slide step while holding the bean bag
- Toss the bean bag over their head, clap one time in front before catching the bean bag (five times)
- Seven jumping jacks alternating the bean bag from hand to hand above their head with each jumping jack.
- Toss the bean bag above your head, clap one time behind your back before catching it.
- Five mountain climbers over the top of the bean bag
- To extend the warm-up, have the students partner up. Standing five to ten feet apart, have them toss one bean bag back and forth. Then have them toss both bean bags back and forth at the same time.

Boys and Girls

K-5

Some days I will use the boys and girls warm-up. I will tell them what to do.   The boys will be doing one exercise and the girls a different exercise; sometimes I have them doing the same exercise. An example would be: Boys gallop and the girls skip clockwise. Then I could say boys skip and girls gallop, or boy's walk and girls jog, girls seal walk and boys crab walk, everyone walks backwards. I usually have both boys and girls do the same exercises, but not at the same time. I do not have one group doing a movement exercise, (skipping), with a non-movement exercise (push-ups). You can also have the girls give a high five to the other girls and the boys do a low five. There are a lot of possibilities and the kids enjoy this warm-up a lot. I use this warm-up more with my K – 3 students

Criss Cross Tag

K-5

Equipment needed: Different color bean bags. If you have 25 students you would need five bean bags in each of five colors (five red, five blue, etc).

This can be used as the main activity or as a warm-up activity. Students walk around the gym holding their bean bag. When the teacher calls out a color, the students with that color are it. When a player is tagged they freeze with their hands held up in front of them. They are frozen until another player comes to them to Criss Cross count to ten with them.

TIPS:

- Players should drop their bean bags when Criss Cross counting or spelling.
- Each players counts or spells two at a time (1,2 – then the other 3,4, etc)
- Players cannot be frozen when trying to unfreeze players.
- Taggers may not tag the same player twice in the same game.
- Bean bags are not thrown.
- No running. Remind students to watch where they are going and to stay on their feet.
- You can count by ones, twos, threes, etc. You can also use spelling words or have them spell their names. There are many possibilities.

Deck-Tennis Ring Warm-up

K-3

Equipment needed: 30 to 40 deck tennis rings with a number from 1 to 10 on one side of each ring, and four cones.

Scatter the rings around the center of the gym, inside the four cones, with the numbers facing the floor. When the music starts or on your command have the students move around the outside of the cones, moving in the same direction. They can skip, gallop, jog, slide, etc.

When the music stops or when the whistle blows the students stop and you give them an exercise to perform (push-ups). They go inside the cones to a ring, turn the ring over to see how many times they will do the exercise (push-ups). After they have done the exercise they step back to the outside of the cones and wait for you to start them again. They may not go to the same ring twice. I also remind them to be careful when going to a ring since people are coming from different directions.

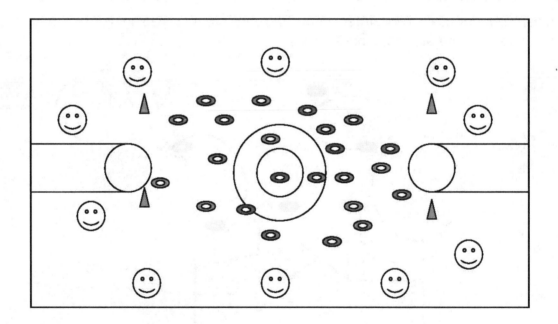

Foam Frisbee Fun

K-3

Equipment needed: Foam Frisbees (one for each person) with numbers written on the bottom (1-5 or 1-10).

Each student will have a foam Frisbee. When the music is playing or on your command they will travel holding on to the Frisbee (skip, gallop, slide step, walk, walk backwards, seal walk, crab walk). When the music stops or on your command the students will stop and perform the exercise you call out. They will perform the exercise the number of time indicated on the Frisbee. (Example: if they have the number 5 on the Frisbee they will perform each exercise five times). Have them trade Frisbees with another person after each exercise during the activity.

- Skip clockwise — Hold the Frisbee
- Jumping jacks — Frisbee on the ground in front of their feet
- Crab walk — Frisbee is on their stomach or chest
- Crab push-ups — Frisbee is on the ground under them
- Walk counter-clockwise — Hold the Frisbee, or put it on their head
- Ski Jumps — Ski Jump over the Frisbee
- Gallop counter clockwise — Hold the Frisbee
- Seal walk — Frisbee is on their back
- Push-ups — Frisbee is on the ground under their body
- Walk backwards clockwise — Hold the Frisbee, or put it on their head
- Mountain climbers — Frisbee on the ground under them
- Slide step clockwise — Hold the Frisbee
- Toe touches w/Frisbee — Hold the Frisbee, alternate hands

To make this more than a warm-up, add the following activity:

Students find their own space and

- Toss the Frisbee at an angle so the Frisbee comes back to them (I demonstrate how to throw the Frisbee).
- Throw the Frisbee as far as they can. Pick it up and throw it again. They need to have space when they throw and watch out for others when going to get their Frisbee.
- Partner the students up.
- Toss one Frisbee back and forth with your partner (five to ten feet apart).
- Each partner will toss their Frisbee to their partner at the same time.

Hot Potato

Equipment needed: – Something to throw and catch (yarn ball, bean bag, rubber chicken, etc).

    Have the class partner up or get into groups of three. Have them stand five to seven feet apart. You can change the distance they stand apart. Remind them to toss the ball so their partner has a chance to catch it and to try and catch with their hands. If the ball is above the waist, fingers up, below the waist fingers down. I have the students count or say the alphabet, or do spelling words, etc., when they toss. Each toss would be a letter or a number.   Just tell them what you want them to do before they start to toss. The person holding the hot potato when the music stops will have to do an exercise (five jumping jacks, three push-ups, jog one lap, etc.). When the music starts again, or on your signal, students begin to toss the ball back and forth. When the music stops again, or on your signal to stop, the person holding the hot potato will do the exercise you tell them to do. I change the exercise after every third game.

Hula Hoop Warm Up

K-3

Equipment needed: At least one hula hoop for each person in the class, one object to toss in each hula hoop (ball, rubber chicken, catch ball, scarf, foam dice, etc.), four cones and math flash cards.

The warm-up:

Spread the hula hoops out on the floor in the middle of the gym. Place one object to toss in each hoop. Put four cones on the outside of the hoops. When the music starts or on your command have the students move (skip, gallop, etc.) in the same direction, around the outside of the cones. Change the movement and direction each round. When the music stops or on your command the students stop and stand inside a hula hoop. The students pick up the object in their hula hoop and look at the teacher. The teacher holds a flash card, the group yells out the answer. The answer is the number of times the students will toss and try to catch the object. I ask my students to toss above their heads but not up to the ceiling. When they are done the object is placed back on the floor in the hoop. They step to the outside and wait for instructions on which way to go and how they will move for round two of the warm up.

Tips

- I play five or six rounds and move on the outside for 20 to 30 seconds each round.
- I change the direction they move each round (clockwise, counter clockwise).
- STUDENTS should stand in a different hoop every round.
- There is a different object in every hula hoop.
- I use addition flash cards for grades K and 1, subtraction for grade 2, and multiplication for grade 3.
- I don't use any flash cards with an answer above 10.

Example:

Round 1	Skip clockwise	3 + 3
Round 2	Gallop Counter-clockwise	2 + 5
Round 3	Seal walk clockwise	2 + 4
Round 4	Walk Backwards counter clockwise	7 + 1
Round 5	Slide step clockwise	6 + 4

Hula Hoop Warm up

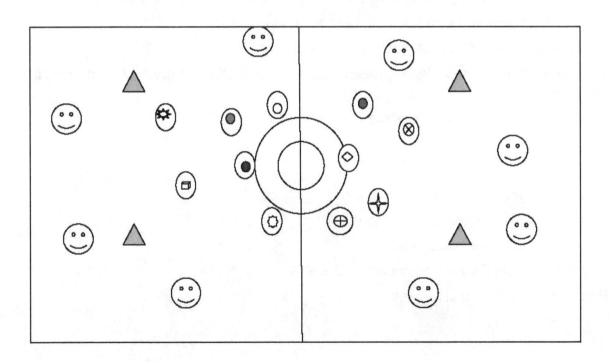

Math & Spelling Cross Crawls

K-5

Equipment needed: Spelling words or sight words, math flash cards.

I try to incorporate cross crawls, spelling or math, into my class each day. An easy way to do this is with spelling or math flash cards. I have the student's partner up or I will give them a partner before we start the warm-up. During the warm-up I will have them stop several times and find their partner to perform a cross crawl, by counting or spelling using their hands with their partners hands. Students have their hands up, palms facing their partner. When they spell or count, partners will take turns crossing the midline of their body with one hand touching their partner's hand, (right hand to right hand, then left hand to left hand). Then the other partner will go. This continues until the word is spelled or the count is finished. Then I will tell them to skip clockwise. When I tell them to stop, or when I blow the whistle, I will tell them to find their partners and cross count the answer to the math problem I am holding up. You can also use sight word flash cards, or get the spelling words for the week from their teacher.

Middle of the Road

K-3

Equipment needed: One yarn ball for each student in the class and poly spots (optional).

Each student has a partner. If you have an odd number there may be a group of three. The partners stand on opposite sides of the road (gym) in front of each other. One partner has a yarn ball for them to throw. One partner throws the yarn ball so that it hits the middle of the road (gym floor) and bounces and rolls to their partner. The partner tries to catch the ball and throw it back the same way, after a few minutes add a second ball. Now both partners have a yarn ball. They need to communicate with each other to throw the ball at the same time. Maybe say 1,2,3 or A,B,C throw. You can also have them communicate without talking. We talk about release point and accuracy when throwing. We also talk about moving their feet to get in front of the ball and keeping knees bent and fingers down when trying to catch the ball.

I use different colored yarn balls so they know which one is theirs. You could put poly spots in the middle on the floor to show them where the middle of the road is.

We are working on throwing form, catching, space awareness and communication.

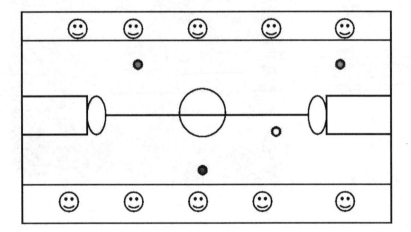

Partners

K-3

Age, height, hair length, shoe size, missing teeth, siblings, eye color.

Some days I have the student's partner up to warm-up. I will tell them the exercise to perform and tell them how long or how many depending on how they match up with their partner. An example would be the partner with the longest hair does five jumping jacks and shortest hair does seven. Find out the age of your partner, that is how many push-ups you will do. Your partners shoe size is how many ski-jumps you will do. The number of missing teeth you have is how many laps you and your partner will jog. Have one partner skip and the other partner walk, then have the walker gallop and the skipper walk, or the walker crab walk and the person galloping seal walk. There are a lot of possibilities with this type of warm-up. I use this warm-up more with my k-3 students.

Poly Spot Warm-Up

K-3

Equipment needed: 30 poly spots, five colors, six of each color (red, green, orange, purple, yellow).

Scatter the different colored poly spots around the gym. When the music starts, or on your command, have the students move in the same direction. They can skip, gallop, jog, slide step, crab walk, etc.

When the music stops, or when the whistle blows, students go and stand on one of the poly spots. Each student will perform the exercise that goes with the color they are standing on five times. Red – Jumping Jacks, Green – Mountain Climbers, Orange – Ski Jumps, Purple – Push-Ups, Yellow – Crab Push- Ups. When the music starts again, or on your command, the students move in the same direction again, using a different movement. When the music stops again, or when the whistle blows, the students go and stand on a different colored poly spot.

They should go to a different color each time.

- Students do not go to the same color twice.
- You can add more spots, more colors and exercises.
- You will probably have to tell them each time what exercise to do at each color.
- You can write the exercises and the color on a dry erase board.

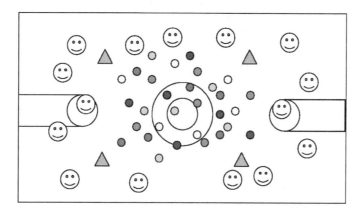

Poly Spot Warm-up

Rock, Paper, Scissors

Have your students find a partner or you give them a partner. The partners will play the game Rock- Paper-Scissors. The students will count one, two, three, and show on three or they can count one, two, three, shoot, and show on shoot. Make the decision as a class before starting the warm-up.

You will tell them what exercise they will perform and how many times they will perform the exercise before they play. After the count the students will show:

A fist is rock, their palm is paper, or two fingers is scissors.

Rock beats scissors, scissors beats paper, and paper beats rock.

Example:

Round one, play two times: Jumping jacks- winner does three, loser does five and if they are the same they both do seven.

Round two, play two times: Push-ups- winner does three, loser does five, the same seven push-ups.

You will decide the number of times they perform the exercise.

Rock

Paper

Scissors
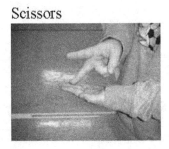

Rock Paper Scissors - Music Notes

K-3

Equipment needed: 60 to 70 laminated music notes and symbols

We use: Staff, Measure, Repeat Sign, Bass Clef, Crescendo, Forte, Treble Clef, Half Note, Quarter Note, Eighth Note, and Whole Note, six of each.

Students are given two cards to start the game. They will travel from student to student playing Rock, Paper, Scissors, with their feet. They jump three times, feet together, saying rock, paper, scissors. On the third jump: If they land with their feet together, that is rock, feet apart, side to side, is paper, feet apart, forward and back, is scissors.

The person who wins will get a music card from the person who lost. They will both go to another person and play again. If a player runs out of music cards they can go to the teacher and get another card. When the teacher runs out of cards a player will have to win a game to get another card.

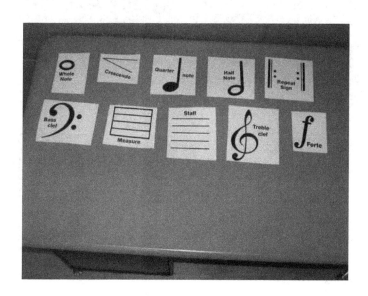

Rock

Paper

Scissors

Rock Paper Scissors & Music

Rock beats Scissors

Roll Call

K-2

Equipment needed: A ball to roll for each group of three, 20 to 30 poly spots.

The game:

Divide the class into groups of three. Give each person in the group a number: one, two, or three. Have number one from each group stand on a poly spot. When the music starts on your command, number two and three will walk together around the gym with the ball. When the music stops, or on your command to stop, they will go to a person standing on a spot, one on each side of the person on the spot, two or three feet away. The person on the spot will open their feet about shoulder width apart over the spot. The ball is rolled between the feet, over the spot to the person standing on the other side. When the ball is rolled the person rolling the ball will say the name of the person standing over the spot. The ball is rolled back the same way. The rollers then move on to another person. This continues until you blow the whistle for them to stop. Before starting a new round, have number two stand on a spot and number one and three will be the rollers. When the music starts, or on your command, number one and three will move around the gym until the music stops, or on your command to stop, they are the rollers. For the next round, have number three stand on a poly spot and continue the activity with number one and two rolling the ball.

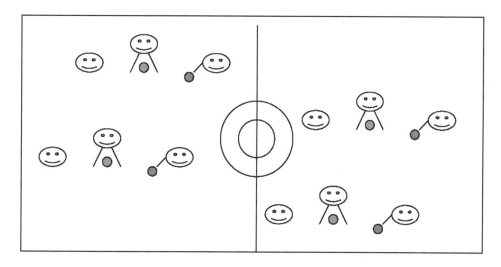

Roll call

31

Share Walk

K-2

Equipment needed: Footballs, rings, foam dice, Frisbees, bean bags etc.

Students walk around the gym in general space with five or six of the students carrying something (football, rings, foam dice, Frisbee bean bags etc.). The students carrying an object must hand it off to the first person passing by them that is not carrying anything. The students do not trade off. They must hand the object to someone that is not carrying anything. Exchanges can happen very quickly as most of the students walking are not carrying an object. This is a continuous activity. You can change the objects being handed off. You can change the way the objects are handed off (only on the right side of your body, or girls can only hand off to boys and boys to girls.) This is a good warm-up. Students must keep their heads up to avoid bumping into each other. They must hold on to the object and not throw it. They also must share the object with anyone, not just one or two people. You may have more or fewer students carrying objects depending on the size of your class.

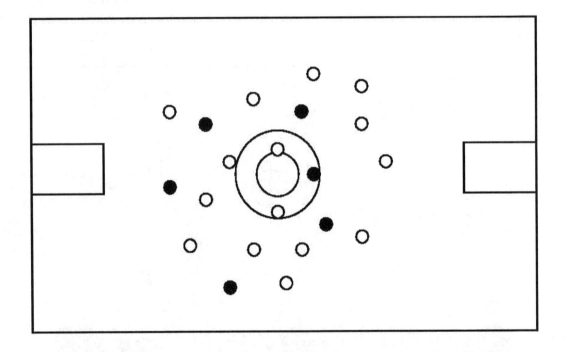

● - Carrying an object.

Soccer Poly Spot Math
(Dribbling)

1st – 3rd

Equipment needed: Soccer balls for half the class, math flash cards, 20 to 30 poly spots

Have each student get a partner. You can have groups of three. Give one partner a soccer ball and the other a math flash card. I use addition for first and second grade and subtraction for third grade. The partner with the flash card shows the card to the dribbling partner. The dribbler answers the problem and dribbles and stops on that number of poly spots. Example: 3 + 2 = 5, the dribbling partner will dribble and stop on five different poly spots. The partners trade the ball and the card. They will trade their flash card with another set of partners or they can trade their card with the teacher. The partner with the flash card needs to watch or follow the dribbler to make sure they stop on the correct number of poly spots.

Chapter 2
Integrated Games

Animal Control

Equipment needed: 30 cones (12" or 18"), laminated pictures of animals (one for each cone, six squirrels, six raccoons, six snakes, four skunks, four armadillos, two bobcats, and two alligators), eight hula-hoops, four poly-spots.

The Set-up: Divide the class into four teams. Each team will be lined up behind a poly-spot, ten to fifteen feet from the cones, in their own section of the gym. Give each team two hula-hoops: one to roll, 24", and one to put their animals (cones) in, 36". The animals, (cones) are scattered in the center of the gym.

Objective: To roll the hula hoop and trap the animals, by having the hoop land around the cone.

The Game: The first person on each team will roll their hoop (24") and try to have it fall around one of the animals, (cones). If the hula hoop does land around one of the animals (cones), they take the trapped animal back with them. The hoop is given to the next person in line and the cone is placed in the hoop (36") on the floor behind the team. If their hoop does not trap an animal then they just get the hoop and give it to the next person in line. Play for three to five minutes. Have the teams rotate after each game. The team with the most points wins the game.

Points:

Squirrels	2 Points
Raccoons	3 points
Snakes	4 points
Skunks	5 points
Armadillos	6 points
Bobcats	8 points
Alligators	10 points

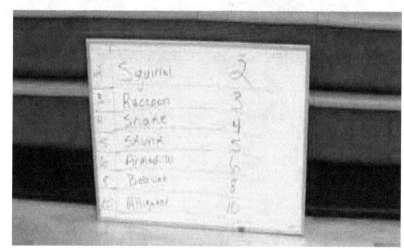

- When the game is over count the points and put the cones back in the center of the gym.
- Have the teams rotate clockwise to a new spot after each game.
- They must roll the hoop, no throwing.
- If you can, have one color of hula hoops for each team, with a matching color poly spot for them to stand behind.
- Put a piece of tape or a poly spot under each cone so you know where to put the cones when starting a new game.
- If you have four-squares painted on your gym floor, use them to put the cones in instead of a hula hoop. Tape a large square on the floor.

- Use a dry erase board to display the animal names and how many points they are worth when caught.
- Each group could use a small erase board and pen to count up their points.
- You might use more cones or use different animals.
- The pictures could be taped to Frisbees instead of cones.

Animal Control

Animal Control

Animal control

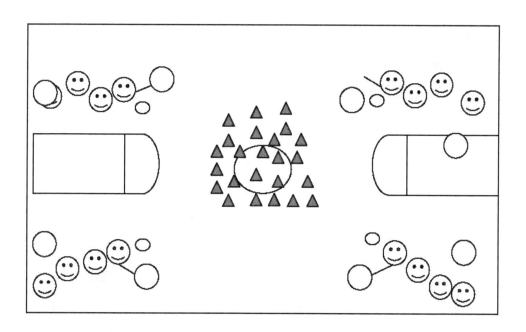

Color Wheel

2nd – 3rd

Equipment needed: Cones or Frisbees, crayons or colored pencils (one for each color in the color wheel), one paper with five color wheels on it, and a list of the colors they will find in order for each team. Five names of artists to tape on the cones (optional). Our art teacher has selected twelve colors for the color wheel. There are three primary colors, three secondary colors, and six intermediate colors.

   Divide the class into teams of three to five people. Each team will stand behind their cone. The first person will take the color wheel paper and travel out to find the first color on their color wheel. They will look under the cone or Frisbee until they find the color. When they find the color they will put the paper on the floor and call their team out, and each person will color in one section of their wheel. They will put the color back under the cone or Frisbee, and go back to their cone and give the paper to the next person in line. The first team to find all of their colors, and color in the wheels on their paper, wins the game.

- Only the person with the paper can be out looking for a color.
- The colors must be found in the order listed on their paper.
- Each person colors in their own color wheel.
- Have each member of the team write their name under one of the color wheels on their paper. If you can write their names before class it will save time.
- Number the names so they know the order to travel out and look for the colors
- There will be people moving in different directions so they need to watch out for each other when going to and from the colors.
- Some colors look alike so they need to read the name of the color on the crayon.
- White construction paper could be used in place of printing paper.
- See reproducible chapter for color wheel.

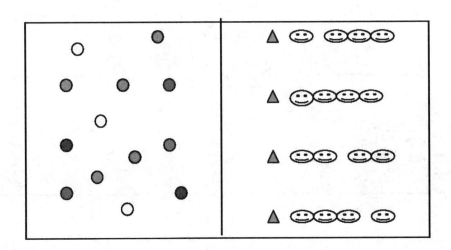

Color Wheel

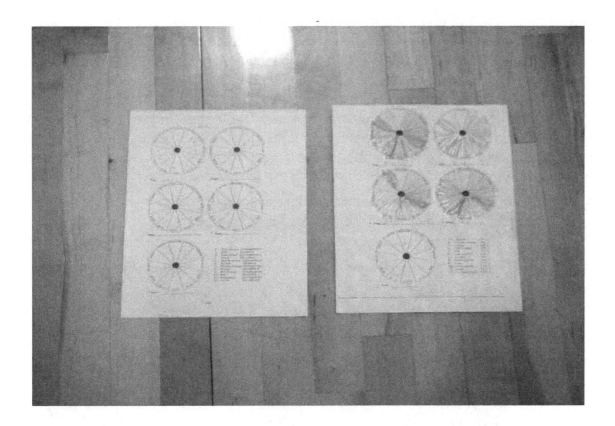

Dice Kickers

K-5

Equipment needed: one or two Foam Dice per group

Singles – one numbered foam dice / groups of three to five people

Have groups lined up single file about 10 feet away from a wall. Tape an x on the floor to show where the dice is set. The groups line up about three feet away from the dice. The first person kicks the dice toward the wall. The number it stops on is their number for that game. The dice is placed back on the x and the next person kicks. This is done until everyone in the group has a chance to kick. In the first game, the person with the lowest number wins. Round two, this time the person with the highest number wins. Round three, this time have them add the numbers together, or subtract from a number you give them, say 35. When they get to zero the round is over.

(Example: 1st person kicks 3, 2nd person 1, 3rd person 4, 3 + 1 + 4 = 8. After the third round start the next round with the low number winning the game.

Doubles – two numbered foam dice / groups six to ten people

We have the groups line up in two single file lines, with the teams about five feet apart, about ten feet away from a wall. There is an x taped on the floor in front of each team where the dice is set. The first person from each team kicks their dice towards the wall. When the dice stops the person with the lowest number wins. The dice is placed back on the x and the next two players kick. (Do not let one team get ahead of the other; each person should be kicking against an opponent.) Play until each player has a chance to kick. The team with the most wins will win the game. In round two the high number wins. In round three have each team add their numbers together; the team with the highest number or the lowest number wins (decide high or low before the start of round three). Start the next round with the lowest number winning again.

In round three you can also give the teams a number, say 50, and have them subtract from that number with each kick. The team with the highest number left wins.

Dice Kickers

Dice Kickers

Dice Kickers Graphing

K-5

Equipment needed: One or two Foam Dice per group, Graphing worksheet, crayon (blue or red)

Singles – One numbered foam dice, or one red and one blue dice / groups of four to six people.

Have groups lined up single file about ten feet away from a wall. Tape an x on the floor to show where the dice is set. The group lines up about three feet away from the dice behind the tape line on the floor. The first person in line is the kicker and kicks the dice toward the wall. When the dice comes to a stop, the last person in line, the writer, will color a square for the number in the first empty box. The dice is placed back on the x by the kicker and the next person in line is now the kicker and kicks the dice. The kicker becomes the writer and colors the square for the number the dice landed on. The activity can be done for a set amount of time or until one number on the graph is completely filled up.

You can also use one red dice and one blue dice and alternate kicking the dice. I have a desk to set the graph and colors on by the wall next to this activity.

Doubles – two numbered foam dice

You can play the same game with two foam dice, one red and one blue. You will have two teams kicking at the same time. One team will kick the red dice and one team the blue dice. Each team will have a graphing worksheet and a crayon, red for the red dice and blue for the blue dice. Other colors can be used. See reproducible chapter for graphing worksheet.

You may have questions at the bottom of the graph to answer.

How many times was number 1 landed on for Blue / Red   _____ _____

How many times was number 2 landed on for Blue / Red   _____ _____

How many times was number 3 landed on for Blue / Red   _____ _____

How many times was number 4 landed on for Blue / Red   _____ _____

How many times was number 5 landed on for Blue / Red   _____ _____

How many times was number 6 landed on for Blue / Red   _____ _____

What number was landed on the most for Blue / Red   _____ _____

Dice Kickers Math

K-5

Equipment needed: Foam Dice, pencil, Dice Kicker math sheet (reproducible chapter).

   Singles – First person kicks, they write their number down in the first box. The second person kicks and they write their number down in the next box and they add the numbers together and write the answer in the third box. The next person kicks and they write their number in the first box on the next line, etc.

   You can also do subtraction and multiplication. See reproducible chapter for paper used for writing the numbers down. In kindergarten have them write down the number kicked on the paper under the correct column (see reproducible chapter).

   I like to use this activity when we are doing station activities. It is a great way to integrate math.

5	+	4	=	9
6	'+	1	=	7
3	'+	2	=	5

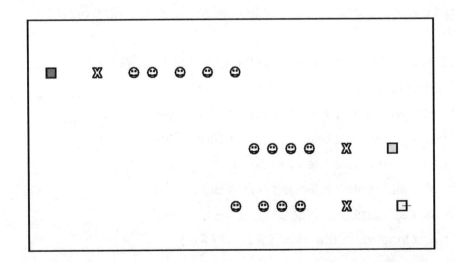

Dribble Math

1st-3rd

Equipment needed: One basketball for each student, 26 - 52 poly spots, each poly spot with one number on it. You can have spots with duplicate numbers.

The poly spots are scattered around the gym on the floor. Have each student get a basketball, place it on one of the spots, and stand over it.

Have the students pick their basketball and dribble around so they can see where the numbers are in the gym.

Have them partner up. They will need one basketball. I give each pair six to ten addition math flash cards to use. The person dribbling picks a card, the partner holds it. The dribbler then dribbles to each number in the problem, and then to the answer, with the partner staying with them. When they finish, the partner should tell if they have the correct answer. They switch and the other partner becomes the dribbler and selects another card. If a pair finishes their stack of flash cards, you can have them switch cards with another pair.

- You can use subtraction, multiplication, or division flashcards. Be sure to have numbers on the spots to match the numbers on the flash cards.
- You decide which hand they dribble with.
- They should watch where they are going. There is a lot of movement with this activity and they need to be under control.

Dribble Math

Dribble Math

Dribble Spelling

1st – 3rd

Equipment needed: One basketball for each student, 26 - 52 poly spots, each poly spot with one letter of the alphabet. You can have more spots with duplicate letters.

The poly spots are scattered around the gym on the floor. Have each student get a basketball, place it on one of the spots, and stand over it.

- Have the students pick their basketball and dribble around so they can see where the letters are in the gym.

- Have them dribble spell their first name. They dribble around when they get to the first letter in their name they dribble one time on that letter and then go to do the rest of the letters in their name. When they finish they can start on their last name or do their first name again, until everyone has finished spelling their name.

- Have them partner up. They will need one basketball. I give each pair five sight word flash cards to use. The person dribbling picks a card, the partner holds it. The dribbler then dribbles to each letter in the word to spell it, with the partner staying with them. When they finish spelling the word they come to me, show me the card and say the word (optional). They switch and the other partner becomes the dribbler and selects another card. If a pair finishes their stack of flash cards you can have them switch cards with another pair. You can also put spelling words on 3 x 5 cards to use.

Tips

- You can decide which hand they dribble with.

- They should watch where they are going. There is a lot of movement with this activity and they need to be under control.

- You could use alphabet bean bags; they can dribble next to the letter instead of on the letter.

- You can also use flash cards with letters on them and tape the letters on the wall and have them dribble to the letters on the wall.

Dribble Spelling

Letters on the wall

45

Flashcard Dribbling

K-2

Equipment needed: one basketball for each set of partners, ten flashcards for each set of partners.

Have your students get a partner. Give one partner a basketball and the other partner ten flashcards. The partner with the flashcards holds up the problem (7 + 3). The partner with the basketball answers the problem by dribbling the answer, stationary, (10). The flashcard partner is counting as the number of dribbles. If the answer is wrong, give the dribbler one more try; if the answer is correct then the partners will switch roles. All of the partners should be spread out in the gym so they have their own space. If they finish their stack of flashcards they can trade with another group.

Another way to play is to give all the students a basketball to dribble. The teacher has the flashcards. The teacher holds up a flashcard and all of the students dribble the answer while moving around the gym. You can have them dribble with their left hand, right hand, alternate hands, it is up to you. Remind the class to keep their heads up and eyes open and watch where they are going.

Tips:

- This activity can be used with higher grades, (3rd-5th) using multiplication or division.
- This could also be a warm-up activity.

Flashcard Dribbling

46

Four point Tee Ball

1ˢᵗ-3rd

Equipment needed: Whiffle ball bat, 6" or 7" gator skin ball, T-ball tee, 4' x 8' mat (optional), four cones

You can use a smaller ball or a yarn ball.

Divide the class into groups of four to six people. Each group will have one bat, one tee, one ball, one mat, four cones. When using the 6" or 7" gator skin ball, I like to take the tube out of the tee and use the rubber piece connected to the base, because the ball sits better on that piece. This will make the tee shorter, so I set the tee on a folded mat. You could use the tee and a big bopper to hold the ball. I set the first two cones up 25 to 30 feet from the tee and the next two cones 35 to 40 feet away from the tee. The cones are about 20 feet apart (width). With a group of six people, you will have one batter and one person on deck. Two people will stand between the four cones that were set up, and two people behind the last two cones.

Scoring for the batter:

1 point for a ball that stops before it reaches the first two cones.

2 points for a ball that is stopped between the first four cones.

3 points for a ball that passes the first four cones but is stopped before it hits the wall.

4 points for a ball that hits the back wall.

0 points for a ball that is caught in the air (the batter is out).

1 point for a ball that is hit and goes outside the cones (foul ball).

Rotation:

After the first person bats he changes places with the on-deck batter. When both are done batting, they go to the three point area. The people in the three point area go to the two point area, and the people in the two point area go in to bat. If there are five people in a group the person by themselves does not bat twice. If there are four people in a group, you will have two batters and one person in the two point area and one in the three point area. When the two batters finish, they switch places with the two fielders.

Players will keep track of their own score and add up their score each time they bat.

Tips:

- The batter needs to hold on to the bat.
- The on deck batter must stay away from the person batting.
- All defenders must be ready to catch the ball.
- Set up two or three games in the gym.
- You can rotate players to the next field after about seven minutes; start the new game with zero points.
- You can use a different color ball or a different size ball or a different ball (Eurofoam ball) at each field.

Four point T-Ball

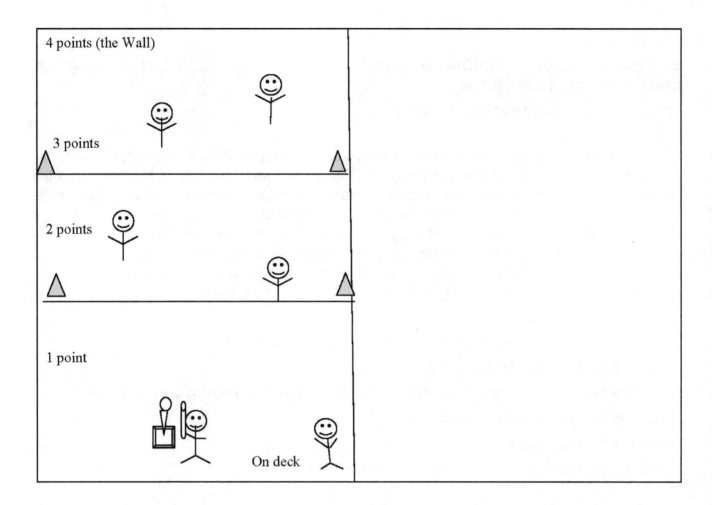

4 points (the Wall)

3 points

2 points

1 point

On deck

Hoop Spelling

4th-5th

Equipment needed: One basketball for each shooting group, one poly spot for each shooting spot. Get a list of spelling words from their teacher.

This is a great game for a lot of shooting.

Mark four or five spots on the floor around the basket. Divide the class into teams of three or four people. Give each team a basketball and assign them a spot to shoot from. Choose a word from their spelling list for that week. On your command to go, the first person from each team shoots from their spot. They get one shot and they rebound their own shot, then give the basketball to the next person in line. Every shot made is a letter in the word they are spelling. The first team to spell the word by making shots sits down. I ask that team to spell the word together. If they spell the word correctly they are the winner. If they misspell the word, then the game continues, without that team shooting.

Teacher tips:

- We talk about shooting form before we start the activity. Square to the basket, eye on the basket, use their legs (jump), and follow through. Take a good shot.
- You can use tape instead of poly-spots, but the poly spots are easier to move if you want to change a shooting spot.
- Remind them to watch out for the other basketballs being shot so they don't get hit.
- Start with smaller words if that is an option.
- I have the teams say the letter (loud) when they make a basket.
- I have them rotate to the next spot for each new game.
- Vary the distance of the spots.
- Have larger teams of five people.
- I only have two goals; use more if you have them.

Variation: After four or five words I have teams on each half of the gym work together. When a shot is made by any team on one half of the gym it is a letter for all teams on that half. It is important that the letter is yelled out when a basket is made so that the teams working together know what letter they are on when spelling the word. Using longer words is better for this game.

Hoop Spelling

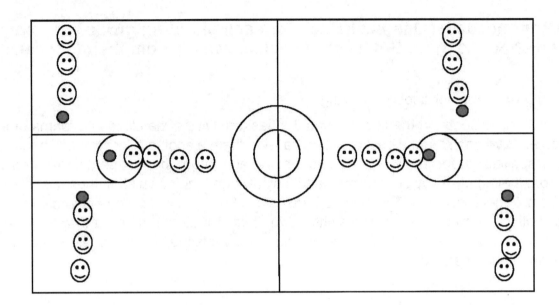

Inside/Outside Vocabulary and Math

K-3

Equipment needed: 20 to 30 poly spots, rings, math problems and vocabulary words written on 3x5 cards, 20 to 30 objects to toss and catch (one for each ring), four to six cones.

Set up: Place the cones in the gym to form a square or rectangle. Inside the square or rectangle, spread the poly spots out on the floor. Put one vocabulary or spelling word on each spot and put one math flashcard on top of the word. The words should be written on 3 x 5 cards. Place one ring next to the poly spot with a ball or other object to toss and catch on the ring.

Have the students get a partner; if there is an odd number there can be a group of three. When the music starts, or on your command, the students will move around the outside of the cones. You can have them skip, gallop, walk, etc. When the music stops the students go inside the cones (they are not using their partner yet), stand by one of the poly spots and pick up the object to toss and catch. The number of times they toss and catch is determined by the answer to the math flashcard. When they finish at one spot they will go to another spot until the music starts again (1 to 1 ½ minutes). When the music starts they will go outside the cones to skip, gallop, walk, etc. When the music stops they go inside again. Do this two or three times and then have them toss and catch with their partner. Each partner should be two or three feet away from the spot. After doing the math two or three times, have them spell the words while tossing and catching. When the partners get to a spot they will take the word and put it on top of the math flashcard. Each toss is a letter in the word. When they finish one word they move to the next spot to spell another word until the music starts again.

Example:

Round:				
1	Skip 20 to 30 seconds	Toss to self 1 to 1 ½ minutes	"	(math)
2	Walk 20 seconds	Toss to self 1 to ½ minutes	" "	(math)
3	Gallop 20 to 30 seconds	Toss to self	" " " "	(math)
4	crab walk 15 seconds	Toss w/ partner	" " " "	(math)
5	walk backwards 10 secs	Toss w/ partner	" " " "	(math)
6	seal walk 15 seconds	Toss w/ partner	" " "	(spelling)
7	Jumping jacks 10 seconds	Toss w/ partner	" " "	(spelling)
8	Walk 20 seconds	Toss w/ partner	" " "	(spelling)
9	Push ups 15 seconds	Toss w/ partner	" " "	(spelling)

Tips:

- Don't toss the object too high when tossing it to yourself.
- Don't be in a big hurry; make a good toss and try to catch it every time.
- Be a good partner. Make a good toss to your partner, something they can catch. Not wild, hard, fast, high or low.
- Use spelling words or vocabulary words from the classroom if possible.
- Watch out for others when going from spot to spot.

Inside/Outside Vocabulary and Math

Inside/Outside Vocabulary and Math

Kick and Spell Kickball

1ˢᵗ – 3rd

Equipment needed: One kickball (8" playground ball, or Nerf soccer ball), two home plates, one base, two large, different colored hula hoops, numbered pinnies for the teams are optional and flash cards for the words the teams will spell.

Divide the class into two teams with eight to ten people on a team. There are two home plates, one for the catcher and one for the kicker. The pitcher slowly rolls the ball to the kicker. When the ball is kicked, the kicker runs to the base on the other side of the gym. I use the half circle at the top of the lane as my base. The teacher stands at the base and hands a card with a letter on it to the runner. The runner touches the base, takes the card and runs back to the plate that they kicked from. If the runner can touch home plate before the catcher can get the ball and touch their own home plate, then the runner is safe. After touching home, the runner puts the card, letter facing up, in their team's hula hoop. The fielding team gets the ball and throws it to their catcher. If the catcher has the ball and touches his team's plate before the runner can get back to their plate, then the runner is out. Even if the runner is out they still put their card in the hula hoop. Each word is three letters long. After the first three kickers, the team should arrange the letters to make the word. The next three kickers will make the next word. You can give a kicker two letters if needed.

The team receives one extra point for each word spelled correctly.   When all the players have kicked, the teams switch places. I like to use numbered pinnies so the teams know their batting order and to spread them out on defense. Using pinnies makes it easier to rotate positions on defense.

- You can rotate defensive positions after each kicker so all players have a chance to be the pitcher and the catcher
- I bought a deck of three letter cards with pictures on them to use.
- You could also use rhyming words, synonyms, or antonyms.
- Alphabet bean bags could be used.
- Use two different colors for the hula hoops. If the teams are red and blue, use a red and blue hula hoop.

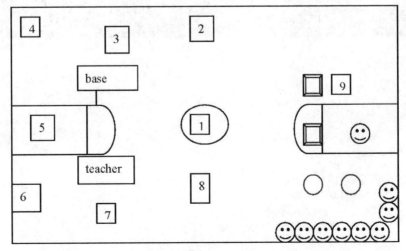

- Defense 1 – 9 can rotate 1 to 2, 2 to 3… 8 to 9, 9 to 1. You could also rotate the opposite way 9 to 8, etc.
- We rotate after each kicker, so there is a new pitcher for each new kicker.

Rhyming words 3rd grade

3 Letter words 1st and 2nd grade

Magnetic Spelling

K – 5

Equipment needed: Eight to twelve sets of magnetic alphabets, four of the following: small magnetic boards, 20 + Frisbees, jump ropes, basketballs, balloons, juggling scarves, cones, deck tennis rings, and four hula hoops.

Divide the class into four teams, three to five people on a team. Place one cone and one team at each corner of the gym with a deck tennis ring on it. Place a hula hoop on one side of the cone. The player waiting to go will stand by the cone. Put the board and the hula hoop at the back of the line. Put the jump rope, basketball, juggling scarf, and balloon in the hula hoop. Put one Frisbee for each team on the large circle at half court. The Frisbees will hold the letters for the word to be spelled. In the first game, everyone will skip to their Frisbee. The person going must carry the deck tennis ring. On your signal, the first person will skip to the Frisbee and pick up one letter. They will skip back to the line, give the next person the ring, and place the letter on the board. Each person will do this until all the letters are gone. When all the letters have been collected each team should put the letters together and try to spell the word you have chosen. If the word was **cards,** then they would be trying to spell the word **cards.** When a team thinks they have spelled the correct word, they should sit down in line. The first team to spell the word correctly wins. When all the teams are done, start a new game. The last person in line should take the Frisbee with the letters back to you. Each game has a new skill when traveling to the letters. Set up a new Frisbee with the letters for the next word in them and start the next game.

2nd game - dribbles the basketball to the letters, leave the deck tennis ring on the cone

3rd game – gallop to the letters

4th game – jump rope to the letters, leave the deck tennis ring on the cone

5th game – slide step to the letters

6th game – pushes a balloon with their hands to the letters, leave the deck tennis ring on the cone

7th game – walk backwards to the letters

8th game – toss and catches a juggling scarf with one hand to the letters, leave the deck tennis ring on the cone

9th game – walk to the letter

Tips:

- Have several words ready to go by using more than one Frisbee for each team.
- Have eight to twelve sets of letters.
- You could use spelling words, words from a book they are reading in class, words from a science or history unit, words they are using in music, art or in PE.

56

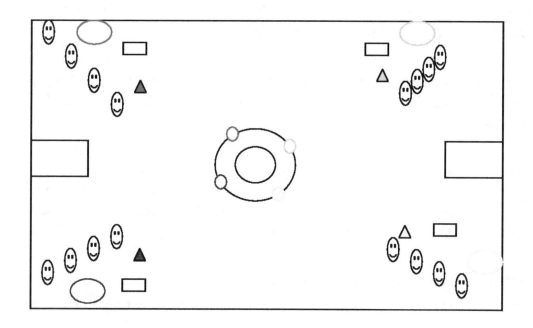

Math Punters

2nd – 3rd

Equipment needed: 40 to 50 foam footballs, 8" or larger gator skin or euro-foam balls, math flash cards, four 4x8 tumbling mats, floor tape if needed, scoreboard (optional). Nerf footballs could be used.

Set up: Divide the class into two teams with one team on each side of the gym. Use the tumbling mats to make a box in the center of the gym. Give each team half of the punting balls. Players will start in the designated punting zones.

The game: The teacher will hold up a flash card (5 + 7), both teams working together will try to punt twelve balls into the box in the center of the gym. The students may go in the no- punting zone to retrieve a ball, but must punt it from the designated punting zone. The teacher will keep track of how many punted balls make it into the box.

- Students may only punt from the punting zones
- Students need to watch out for punted balls and the people that are punting them
- A time limit can be set for each round
- A flip scoreboard or an electronic scoreboard may be used
- Use flashcards appropriate for each class, addition, subtraction, multiplication, division
- Using two mats instead of four mats will increase the difficulty

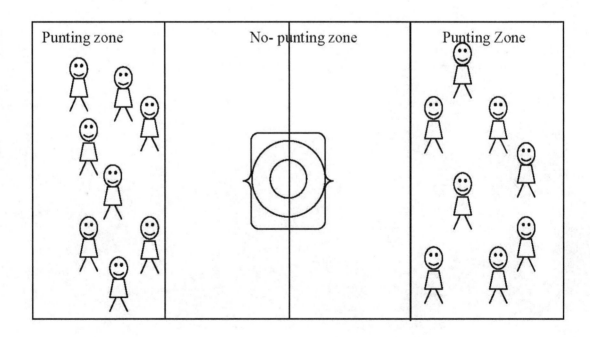

Math Rollers

Equipment needed: 20 – 50 poly spots with numbers on them, one yarn ball per group, math flash cards (ten per group)

Divide the class into groups of three people. Each group has one yarn ball or another ball to roll, and ten flash cards. One partner shows a flashcard. The partner with the ball answers by finding the poly spot with the correct answer on it and rolling the ball over it to the third partner. Partners should stay together. If you have groups of two, the ball will be rolled over the spot to the partner with the cards. If the ball is rolled over the wrong answer, the other partner should tell them, show them the problem and give them another chance to roll the ball over the correct answer. Switch rolls after each turn.

Tips:

- You can use addition, subtraction, division, multiplication depending on the age level of the class.
- After a few minutes have the groups trade flash cards.
- Make sure the answers to flashcards are not higher than the number of poly spots you have. If you have poly spots numbered 1 to 30 you should not have any answers higher than 30.

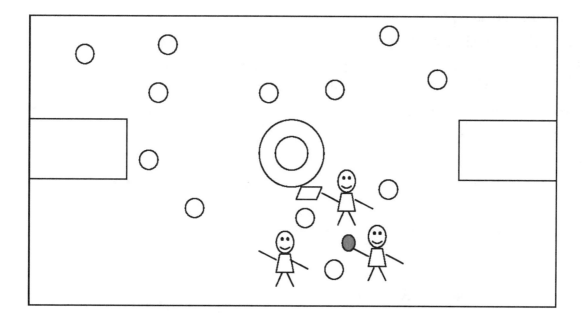

Music Notes

K-3

Equipment needed: Music notes and symbols copied, laminated and cut out, Frisbees to tape the notes on, one cone for each team to stand behind. Each team will have a deck tennis ring to carry when looking under the Frisbees. Each cone will have a Picture of the music note they are looking for taped to it. Each team will have a hula hoop at the end of their line to put their Frisbee with the music note or symbol on it when they find it.

Divide the class into teams of four or five. Each team will be given a deck tennis ring. The first person will take the ring and travel to the Frisbees and try to find their music note. They will turn one Frisbee over. If they find their note or symbol they will bring it back with them and put it in their hula hoop and give the ring to the next person in line. If they do not find their note they put the Frisbee back like they found it and go back to give the ring to the next person in line. The first team to find their five notes or symbols wins the game.

- Only the person with the ring can be looking for notes
- You will need several copies of each note. I use six of each. Each team finds five, and one is taped to the cone.
- Take the Frisbee with them when they find their note or symbol
- I have ten music notes or symbols.
- I use five notes or symbols the first game and five in the second game.
- If you do not have enough Frisbees, just cover the note with the Frisbee and they can take the note and leave the Frisbee turned over on the floor.
- If you have ten copies of each, you could play Rock Paper Scissors Music as a warm-up (find in the warm up chapter of this book).
- See reproducible chapter for notes.
- Using cone covers would be better than taping the notes to the cones.

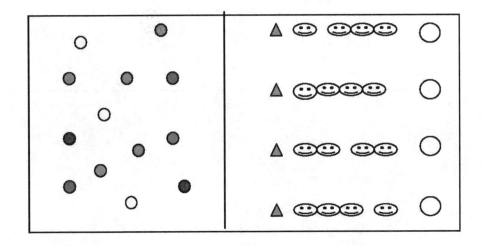

Music Notes

Music Notes

61

Music Notes

Music Notes

Noodles

K-1

Equipment needed: Pool Noodles cut twelve to fourteen inches in length. Try to get different colored noodles. Print letters and numbers toward the end of each noodle. Write a letter on one end and a number on the other end. (Use a permanent marker).

Give each student a noodle and have them find their own space.

1. Balance the noodle on your hand (the end of the noodle is on the hand)
2. Balance the noodle with the noodle laying across the back of your hand
3. Put your index finger in one end of the noodle.
   - Make a plus sign (+) with another person (also a small t)
   - Make a multiplication sign (x) also a small x
   - Make an equal sign (=)
   - Make the capital letter (T, E, F,V, K)
4. Find the person with the same number on their noodle that you have
5. Take the noodle off your finger and stand it up on the floor
6. Try to balance your noodle on top of your partner's noodle
7. Lay your noodle across your foot and kick it up to yourself.
8. Lay your noodle across your foot and kick it up to your partner (stand three to four feet apart).
9. Stand the noodle on end and kick the noodle to your partner who is twelve to fifteen feet away.
10. Have both partners kick their noodle to their partner at the same time.
11. Stand three to four feet apart and toss one noodle back and forth with your partner. The noodle is vertical, not horizontal
12. Stand three to four feet apart and toss both noodles to your partner (keep the noodles in front of your body). Your partner will try to catch one noodle in each hand.
13. Stand three to four feet apart. Each partner has a noodle. Both partners hold the noodle with their right hand and toss it to your partner's left hand. (Count to three and toss the noodle to your partner's open hand.) Repeat by tossing with the left hand to the open right hand of your partner.

Noodles

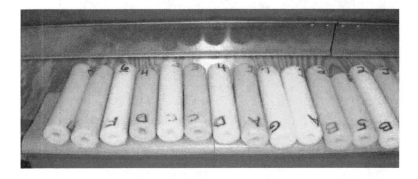

Noodles

Password

3-5

Equipment needed: 15 to 20 deck tennis rings, basketballs, cones and index cards.

Spread out the cones in the gym. Tape the 3 x 5 index cards, with vocabulary words written on them, to the cones. Place a basketball on a ring next to each cone. Have the students get a partner. You could also do groups of three. Show the class what basketball pass they will be practicing, and how to do it (chest pass). On your command, partners will go to a cone, pick up a basketball and spell the word on the cone while performing the chest pass. Each pass is a letter in the word they are spelling. Example: the word DOOR. The first pass they say D the next pass O the next pass O the last pass R. After they have completed the word, the partner with the basketball puts the ball back on the ring, and they move to another word. After two or three minutes have them stop. Show the class the next pass (bounce pass), and they continue.
Tips:

- Before starting we talk about being a good partner and making a good pass, a pass that your partner can catch (not too hard, not wild).

- We talk about how to correctly catch a pass with hands in the proper position: Above the waist fingers up, and below the waist fingers down. Relax the elbows and bring the ball in.

- Partners should take their time, it is not a race.

Password

Password

Percentage Bowling

4th – 5th

Equipment needed: Bowling pins and ball for each lane, percentage bowling score sheet and pencil, Calculator at each lane optional.

Each year during our bowling unit we have one day of percentage bowling. Everything is the same as regular bowling except the way the score is kept. The person keeping score writes down the total number of pins knocked down in a frame over 10 (8/10 80%). The total at the end of the game is the total number of pins knocked down over the total number of pins possible. The score sheet below is an example. There is a score sheet for percentage bowling in the reproducible chapter.

Name	1		2		3		4		5		6		7		8		9		10		total	
	/10	%	/10	%	/10	%	/10	%	/10	%	/10	%	/10	%	/10	%	/10	%	/10	%	/	%
	/10	%	/10	%	/10	%	/10	%	/10	%	/10	%	/10	%	/10	%	/10	%	/10	%	/	%
	/10	%	/10	%	/10	%	/10	%	/10	%	/10	%	/10	%	/10	%	/10	%	/10	%	/	%
	/10	%	/10	%	/10	%	/10	%	/10	%	/10	%	/10	%	/10	%	/10	%	/10	%	/	%
	/10	%	/10	%	/10	%	/10	%	/10	%	/10	%	/10	%	/10	%	/10	%	/10	%	/	%

Name	1		2		3		4		5		6		7		8		9		10		total	
	/10	%	/10	%	/10	%	/10	%	/10	%	/10	%	/10	%	/10	%	/10	%	/10	%	/	%
	/10	%	/10	%	/10	%	/10	%	/10	%	/10	%	/10	%	/10	%	/10	%	/10	%	/	%
	/10	%	/10	%	/10	%	/10	%	/10	%	/10	%	/10	%	/10	%	/10	%	/10	%	/	%
	/10	%	/10	%	/10	%	/10	%	/10	%	/10	%	/10	%	/10	%	/10	%	/10	%	/	%
	/10	%	/10	%	/10	%	/10	%	/10	%	/10	%	/10	%	/10	%	/10	%	/10	%	/	%

Name	1		2		3		4		5		6		7		8		9		10		total	
	/10	%	/10	%	/10	%	/10	%	/10	%	/10	%	/10	%	/10	%	/10	%	/10	%	/	%
	/10	%	/10	%	/10	%	/10	%	/10	%	/10	%	/10	%	/10	%	/10	%	/10	%	/	%
	/10	%	/10	%	/10	%	/10	%	/10	%	/10	%	/10	%	/10	%	/10	%	/10	%	/	%
	/10	%	/10	%	/10	%	/10	%	/10	%	/10	%	/10	%	/10	%	/10	%	/10	%	/	%
	/10	%	/10	%	/10	%	/10	%	/10	%	/10	%	/10	%	/10	%	/10	%	/10	%	/	%

Replacement Parts

K-3

Equipment needed: At least one hula hoop for each person in the class, plus two or three extra hula hoops. Put one of each of the following items in each hula hoop. 25 hoops, 25 bean bags, 25 gator skin balls, 25 deck tennis rings, 25 noodles, 25 scoops. You can use other items in the hoops.

Scatter the hula hoops around the gym. Place four or five items inside each hoop: gatorskin ball, scoop, foam noodle, paddle, bean bag, etc. I like to use music. When the music starts, students walk around the gym and pick up one part from a hoop. They carry that part until they find a hoop that is missing that part, then replace that part with the one they have. Then they pick up a part from that hoop and take it to another hoop that is missing that part. Students keep going until the music stops (about 1 ½ to 2 minutes). If a student is holding a part when the music stops, have them find the hoop that is missing that part and replace it. Before starting another round have all the students stand by a hoop. Then have them pick up the bean bag and toss it to themselves for about a minute. Then start the music and start the next round, of replacing parts. When the music stops have them pick up the gatorskin ball and toss it to themselves or maybe they can bounce it off the floor and catch it. After round three, have them toss the bean bag with their hand and catch it with the scoop. After round four, have them have them use the paddle to keep the gatorskin ball up in the air. The ball should be struck so it is about a foot above the paddle. After round five, have them toss the noodle up in the air and catch it. After round six, have them throw the ball up and catch it with the scoop. You can have different objects in the hoop. There are many possibilities.

Roll and Spell

K – 3

Equipment needed: Alphabet bean bags (one or two sets) or poly spots with letters of the alphabet on them. Spread them out on the floor in the gym. One ball for each group to roll. Five to ten site words on index cards per group. I have site word cards, one word on each side, laminated. I try to use words that are two, three, or four letters long. I use longer words for third grade students.

Divide the class into groups of three people. You could have two or four in a group if the numbers are not right for three. Each group has one ball and five to ten sight word flash cards. One partner shows a word to the other two partners. The partners stay together and find the letters that make up the word. When they come to the poly spot or bean bag with the first letter, the partner with the ball and the other partner stand across from each other about two feet away from the letter. The partner with the ball rolls it over the letter to the other partner. That person will keep the ball and they will search for the next letter and repeat the action. They should try to roll the ball over the letter on the spot. It is ok if the ball rolls next to the letter and not directly over it. After the ball is rolled over the last letter in the word, the partner with the flashcards gives them to one of the other partners, who pick a new word to spell.

With older students you could use spelling words and have them spell the word without showing it to them.

Kindergarten: I use letter flash cards. Each group is given five to seven cards to find and roll the ball over. After five – seven minutes I have them come to me, and we have the groups switch cards. They may get some of the same letters, but they may be lower case instead of capitals.

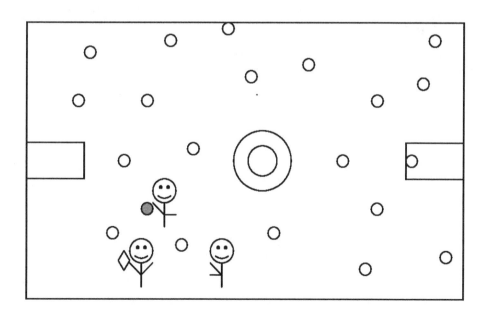

69

States & Capitals

4th grade

Equipment needed: Cones, Deck tennis rings, hula hoops, a map with Numbers, one identification paper with numbers matching the states map. (These are in the reproducible chapter), Index cards- 50 with the name of a state, 50 with the capitals.

   Spread the index cards out into two areas of the gym. One area for the **state** index cards and one area for the **capital** index cards. The states also have the abbreviation written on the back of the index card.

   Split your class into teams of three or four people and place them behind a cone, with a ring on the cone. On your signal to go, the first person in each line takes the ring and travels out to bring back one state card, and places it in the hoop (show the card to the other members of the team before placing it in the hoop). The next person takes the ring and finds the capital that matches the state card that was brought back. The card is shown to the group and placed in the hoop (example, Kansas, Topeka). The next person takes the ring and finds the next state card. Each round will last four or five minutes, around two minutes to pick states and capitals and about two minutes for the groups to write down the state abbreviation and capital on their paper. If the capital card brought back does not match the state card, then the next person in line must take the card back and find the correct card.

Tips:

- Only the person holding the deck tennis ring can be out looking for cards

- Remind them to be in control and to watch where they are going (no sliding)

- You could end a round when a team has four states and capitals in their hula hoop instead having a round last for two minutes.

- When the round is over and they have finished writing, I have them bring the cards to me. I put the cards out and start the next round.

- Having teams of three is great because they stay active and they can stay involved in the writing portion of the activity.

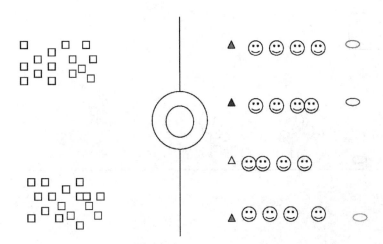

Stomp & Spell

K-2

Equipment needed: Rocket Launchers, two or three sets of alphabet (consonants only) bean bags, alphabet flash cards (vowels only), large hula hoops, mats, deck tennis rings.

Divide the class into teams of four or five. Each team will have a rocket launcher to use, one or two sets of vowels, a deck tennis ring and a hula hoop. The alphabet bean bags are scattered on the floor about 15 feet away, in front of the teams. The hula hoops are on the floor behind the team. The vowels are inside the hoop. The rocket launchers are about 25 feet away.

The first person, holding a deck tennis ring, travels to the alphabet bean bags and picks one up. They take the bean bag to their rocket launcher and place it on the launcher. They can hold the ring or set it down. They step or jump on the rocket launcher and try to catch the bean bag. If they catch the bean bag they take it back to their team's hula hoop and give the deck tennis ring to the next person so they can go. If the bean bag is not caught it is tossed back with the other bean bags. They take the ring to the next person. After 2 minutes, or when all the bean bags have been taken, stop the game. Have each team make as many words as they can with the consonants and vowels they have, using each letter once. Each word must be at least three letters (with Kindergarten you could use two letter words). Give them a few minutes to spell their words. Walk from group to group and help if needed. After you have a chance to check their words (about five minutes), have two people from each group take the bean bags back and start round two. Have one or two people from each team take their letters back to the pile after each game (not the vowels).

I put the rocket launcher on a mat. With each round, I ask the teams to not repeat any of the words they have already spelled. I give each person at least two attempts to catch the bean bag

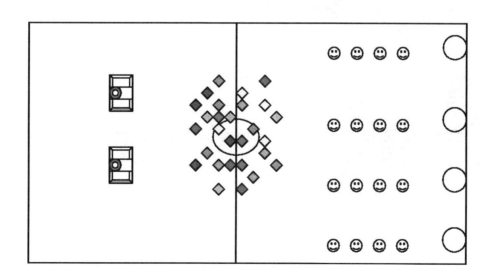

Stomp & Spell

Stomp & Spell

Stomp & Spell

Stomp & Spell

Stomp & Spell

Scavenger Hunt

4th grade

Equipment needed: List of items, clipboards, pencils, a calculator is optional.

I do a scavenger hunt activity with my fourth grade students. I split the class into teams of three. Each team has a clipboard with a paper that has a list of the items and how many points that item is worth if found. Some items are easier to find than others. I hide items in the gym. All of the items are in places where nothing has to be moved or picked up to see the item. I also use some items that are in the gym (badminton birdies stuck in the lights, a sticker with the word "porter" on the backboard). You can do the same in your gym. I also have group exercises and activities as part of the hunt (10 jumping jacks, shoot three shots in the lane). When they do these the whole group has to do them together. They would all do ten jumping jacks, they would all shoot three shots. They do not have to be together when searching for items. I also put some extra credit- type items on the paper. The group can get some extra points if someone in their group is wearing glasses, or if someone has braces, if everyone is wearing tennis shoes, etc.

- I have a copy of my list in the reproducible chapter.
- I leave the last seven or eight minutes to total up the points.

Tips:

- They do not point or yell when they find an item on the list.
- They do not tell the other groups where items can be found.
- Having a calculator for each group at the end of class will speed things up.
- Items easier to find are worth fewer points
- See reproducible chapter for a sample scavenger hunt list.

I have two mats out for sit-ups. I have six jump ropes in one area of the gym, six hula hoops in another area of the gym. I have two volleyballs on deck tennis rings in the lane, at my two basketball goals.

Scavenger Hunt

Scavenger Hunt

Vocabulary Quarterback

3rd – 5th

Equipment needed: Each team will need one football, two poly spots (same color) dry erase board(s) & marker for the teacher

Divide the class into teams of four or five people. The teams will line up behind a poly spot. Have the last person in line go to the poly spot opposite their team. The first person in line will have the football. The teacher will write the vocabulary word on a dry erase board and hold it up so all the teams can see it. Ask the class to say the word. Then set the board down. On the teacher's command to start, the first person will throw the football to their teammate on the poly spot across from them. If the football is caught they will say the first letter of the vocabulary word. If the ball is not caught they do not get a letter in the word being spelled. The thrower becomes the catcher and the catcher takes the ball, hands it off to the next person in line, and then goes to the back of the line. This continues until a team has made enough catches to spell the word. When a team has spelled the word they should sit down. Stop the game and have that team spell the word. If they spell it correctly then the game is over, and we start a new game with the next vocabulary word. If the team does not spell the word correctly, we continue playing the game until another team has made enough catches to spell the word.

- I put the spots about 15 feet apart.
- Do not let the team see the board when they are throwing and catching to spell the word.
- We talk about how the quarterback should hand the ball off.
- I use an 11" x 14" dry erase board.

Vocabulary Quarterback

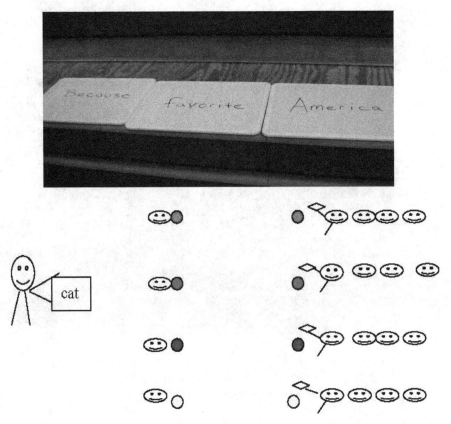

76

Whiffle Ball Buckets

4th – 5th

Equipment needed: Six, 5-gallon buckets, four whiffle balls (two white and tow yellow) for each player. They can be another color. If there are six players use six whiffle balls. Tape numbers on the buckets.

This is a great station activity. Set up the 5-gallon buckets in a pyramid (1, 2, 3). The players will divide up into teams of two, or teams of three if you have six people. They each have a whiffle ball. One team has white and the other has yellow. They will stand single file behind the line, about five feet away, alternating (white team, yellow team, white team, yellow team). They will go one at a time and try to bounce their whiffle ball into one of the buckets. When they all have had a turn, they will retrieve the whiffle balls. They should add up their score after each round. They can play to a set score, or play until time is up at that station, and the team with the most points will win. Each bucket has a different point value.

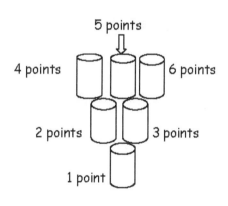

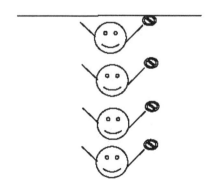

Chapter 3

Games, Lead up Games and Station Activities

Catch 3

K-2

Equipment needed: Ten to fifteen hula hoops, one cone for each hoop, 30 to 45 objects to toss (three in each hoop), numbers to put on each cone.

The Game: Have 10 to 15 hula hoops spread out and lying on the floor. There will be one cone, with a number on it, and three objects to toss inside the hoop. Divide the class into groups of three. Each group of three will be standing around a hula hoop, about two or three feet away from the hoop. When the music starts or on your command to start, one student will pick up one of the objects from the hoop and pass it to one partner, who will pass it to the other partner, who will then pass it back to the first partner. If all three catch the object, it is placed in the hoop, and the first partner will take another object out of the hoop to toss. They do the same thing with all three objects in the hoop. If they catch all three objects successfully, then they will start over with the first object if there is time. The object must be caught by all three partners consecutively before they can pick another object to toss. When the music stops or on your command, the students will stop and move to the next numbered cone. If they start at cone number one, they will move to number two, etc. Students must leave all three objects in the hoop before moving on.

Tips

- Be a good partner. Toss the object so that your partner has a chance to catch it.
- We rotate every two or three minutes. I try to have three different objects at each hoop, even if it is just a different size or shape of the same object in another hoop.
- You may have four people in a group.

Make It -Take It

K-3

Equipment needed: 40 poly spots, eight objects to throw (ball, small rubber fish, bean bag, yarn ball, gatorskin ball, etc.), eight cones, four 18- to 20- gallon utility tubs.

- Divide the class into eight teams, with three or four people on a team. Each team will stand behind a cone. Put the tubs in the middle of the gym, end line to end line. Place two tubs on each half of the gym. There will be one tub between two teams. The first person from each team will take the ball, or other object to throw, go to a spot and try to toss it into the tub. If they make it, then they get the ball and take the spot they were standing on back to their team. If they miss, then they get the ball and give the ball to the next person for their turn. The team that collects all of their spots first wins. The spots are from two feet to ten feet away from the tub.

- Both feet should be on the spot when they toss.

- You can tell them which hand to throw with (left hand only).

- You can have them go in order, starting with the last spot or first spot.

- You can have boys against girls.

- You can set a time limit, one minute, and have every team do an exercise (five ski- jumps) for each spot that is left at the end of one minute.

- Set the distance of the spots to fit your class.

- Put tape on the floor under the poly-spots.

- When one team wins a game have them replace the poly-spots and start a new game.

- Rotate to the next cone every three to five minutes

Make it- Take it

Make it- Take it

What's Under Your Frisbee?

K-5

Equipment needed: one cone for each team to line up behind, 20 to 30 Frisbees, pairs of items to place under the cones, one item under each cone (example two bean bags), one ring for each team, one hula hoop for each team.

Divide the class into teams of five or six people. We usually have three or four teams. The teams line up at one end of the gym. On the other end of the gym, scatter 20 to 30 Frisbees or cones. Under each cone/Frisbee, place a card, picture, or an item like a bean bag. There should be two of a kind of each thing under the cones/Frisbees. Two people from each line go at a time. They jog, skip, gallop or slide step down. When they get to the Cones/Frisbees, they should each turn over one Frisbee or look under a cone. If the items under the cone/Frisbee match, then they leave the cones/Frisbees turned over and take the items back to the end of their line. If the items do not match, then they set the cone/Frisbee back down and go back to the line, and the next two people go. This has been a very fun and popular game for the kids to play.

There are many options for the items under the cones/Frisbees. Math flash cards, parts of speech, states and capitals, money, time clocks, colors, shapes, letters, numbers, music notes, names of bones, Lego blocks, puzzle pieces, state flag, dominoes, balloons, etc.

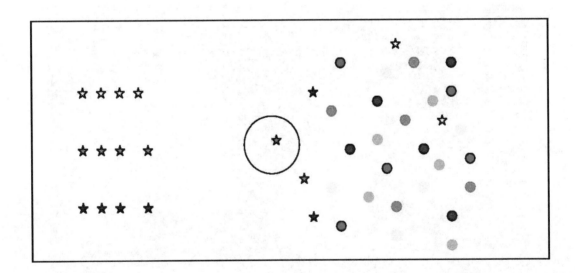

What's under Your Frisbee

What's under Your Frisbee

What's under your Frisbee **team hula hoop**

83

Pig Pin

K – 3

Equipment needed: Foam pins, rubber pigs and a ball to roll for each group.

The Game: The object of the game is to let the pigs out of the pin. Players will roll a ball, kick a ball, throw a ball or roll a ball backwards, trying to knock the pin down and the pig off the pin.

Split the class up into teams of two. The pins, with pigs lying on top, will be placed in the center of the gym. The teams of two, three people if you have an odd number will be standing 15 to 20 feet away on both sides facing the pin. The first person from one team will roll (kick, roll backwards, or throw) the ball at the pin. If they knock the pin down and knock the pig off, they get one point for their team. They will then set the pin back up with the pig on top, and then go stand behind their partner. Then it will be the other team's turn to go. If the person rolling the ball misses the pin, then it is the other teams turn to go. Play for two or three minutes. The team knocking the pin down and the pig off (letting the pig out of the pin) the most will win that game. When time is up, have the players move down one pin and start a new game with a score of zero. There will be a different ball, and a different way of using the ball at each pin. We use a nerf soccer ball, an 8 1/2" gatorskin ball, a ragball soccer ball, a softball size gatorskin ball, a 7" eurofoam ball. I try to have the ball, pig, and poly spot the same color.

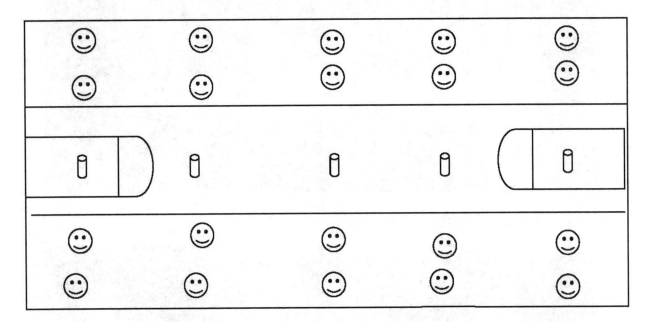

Pig Pin

Kicking - ragball soccer ball

Rolling- Gator skin ball

Rolling backwards-nerf soccer ball

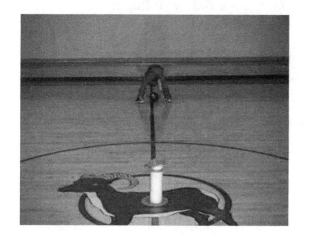

Throwing- gator skin ball

Rolling-eurofoam ball

Pig Pin Set up

Tennis Ball

K-3

Equipment needed: Give each student a tennis ball. I have a letter of the alphabet on each tennis ball so they know which one is theirs.

Stationary: Do each task several times:

- Bounce and catch the tennis ball with the same hand.
- Bounce the tennis ball with one hand and catch it with the other hand
- Bounce the tennis ball and catch it with both hands.
- Bounce the tennis ball, clap hands one time, and catch the tennis ball.
- Bounce the tennis ball, clap hands behind the back, catch the tennis ball in front.
- Bounce the tennis ball, clap hands in front once, behind the back once, catch in front.
- Bounce the tennis ball, clap hands under one leg, catch the ball
- Bounce the tennis ball, clap hands under both legs, one leg then the other leg, catch the ball
- Toss the ball high in the air, let it bounce once, and catch it with both hands

Partners:

- Partners stand about five feet apart and toss one tennis ball back and forth. The ball will bounce once, about half way, before being caught.
- Partners stand about five feet apart. Each has a tennis ball. They will say 1,2,3, go and both will toss (one bounce) the tennis ball to their partner.

Walking:

- Bounce the tennis ball and catch it with the same hand.
- Bounce the tennis ball with one hand and catch it with the other hand.
- Bounce the tennis ball and catch with both hands.

Standing in front of a wall: (<u>I usually do these with grades 1, 2, and 3</u>)

- Stand ten to fifteen feet away from the wall.
- Throw the tennis ball, hit the floor then the wall and catch it.
- Partners – One partner throws the tennis ball (same as above, floor then wall). The other partner catches the tennis ball (2nd & 3rd grade).

Turkey Hunt

K-3

Equipment needed: Two yarn balls for 2/3 of the class, one scooter for 1/3 of the class, one cone for each scooter, one jump rope tied to each scooter, one laminated turkey taped to each cone.

Example: 21 students: 28 yarn balls, 7 scooters, 7 ropes, 7 turkeys

This game is a variation of the "Scooter Shooting Gallery" game submitted by Don Keener in the May 1998 issue of <u>Great Activities</u>. First divide the class into three groups; try to have the same number of people in each group. Two of the groups will be throwers, (hunters), on the sides, and the third group will pull the scooters (turkeys). The throwers stand on either side of the gym. They will be throwing yarn balls, behind a designated line, trying to knock the cones (turkeys) off of the scooter. The cone on the scooter has a laminated picture of a turkey taped to it. The throwers (hunters) may go into the middle of the gym (the woods) to retrieve a ball, but must bring it back behind the designated line to throw the ball. The partner pulling the scooter will start at the end of the gym or at half court. They will **walk,** pulling the scooter behind them down the middle of the gym (the woods). They are trying to walk back and forth as many times as they can without getting their cone (turkey) knocked off. If the cone gets knocked off, they should stop and start walking the opposite direction. A game will last about two minutes. Have the turkeys return to their starting place and have the hunters get two yarn balls each before rotating. I tell the hunters to leave the yarn balls on the line before rotating. I usually rotate clockwise. We usually have time for each group to pull the scooters twice.

Before the game we discuss the proper throwing technique. We also talk about the release point being lower because they are throwing the ball towards the floor. Before each round I remind the students pulling the scooters to walk and watch where they are going because we have people walking back and forth down the middle of the gym.

This game is a lot of fun around Thanksgiving. You could also use pumpkins or ghosts on the cones around Halloween. You could use Leprechauns for St. Patrick's Day.

Tips:

- Remind them to walk and to not swing the scooters around when changing directions. If they go too fast they may trip another student with the rope or hit them with the scooter.

- Hunters going into the middle to retrieve a ball must watch out for the people walking back and forth.

- Hunters must throw from behind the designated line.

- Each hunter will start a new game with two yarn balls; you may have extra yarns balls lying around.

- Turkeys are safe when they are behind the starting line or when they get to half court.

Turkey Hunt

Wands

K - 3

Equipment needed: One plastic wand for each set of partners

1. March.
2. Stretch over head left and right x 2.
3. Behind the back.
4. Down to the toes.
5. Hold the wand low-step over the wand, and back over the wand, hands to the outside.
6. Hold the wand low-step over the wand and back over the wand , hands in the middle.
7. Balance on hand.
8. Balance on wrist or forearm.
9. Balance on shoulder.
10. Balance on head vertical and horizontal.
11. Balance on leg, balance on one foot/switch legs.
12. Balance on the top of the foot, toes raised up- toss the wand up and catch it.
13. Hold the wand in the middle with one hand up, drop to the other hand, down toss it back up and drop back down horizontally.
14. Balance on knees while sitting.
15. Balance on the bottom of a foot or feet while lying down.
16. Crab walk with the wand on the front of your body (stomach).
17. Seal walk with the wand on your back.
18. Partners pass one wand back and forth (close together) vertically.
19. Pass two wands back and forth, 1, 2, 3, go- pass straight across.
20. Wring the dish rag.
21. Lay down on your back, legs straight and arms at your side. Have the partner lay the wands on the floor next to you to see how tall you are, one wand tall, one and a half or two wands tall? Switch places.

Wring the dish rag: Partners face each other with their hands on the wand. One partners hands inside the other outside. They turn the same direction so they go from front to front to side to side, back to back, side to side and back to front to front. Not too fast.

Batting Cages

K - 3

Equipment needed: Batting tees, whiffle ball bats, baseball or softball size gatorskin ball and/or coated nerf ball, or a yarn ball.

There is one batter, and three or four fielders at the opposite side of the gym. The players will number themselves so they know the order they will bat. The batter gets one hit. When the ball is hit, the fielders catch the ball and give it to the next player, who goes to the tee to hit. Having a different ball or a different colored ball at each tee will help each group keep track of the ball they are hitting. I have them rotate to the next tee every five minutes.

Grounders, Pop-Ups, One-Hoppers

K – 3

Equipment needed: gatorskin ball, nerf or poof softball, ragball baseball. Plastic bat, 20-gallon utility tub

Have the students in two lines on one half of the gym. The teacher is in the middle of the gym around the free throw line on the other side of the gym. The teacher has a bat and the tub with the gatorskin balls, poof balls and rag balls in the tub. Hit a ground ball to the first person in one line and then the other. They will catch the ball and bring it to the tub and drop it in. I do this quickly. The students need to be ready and to be in control when going to the tub and back to their line so they do not run into each other. After going through the line two times, I hit pop-flies. After hitting pop-flies I hit one- hoppers. The one-hoppers usually work best with the nerf or poof ball or the small gator- skin ball. This is a fast-paced activity that my kids really enjoy doing.

- It is important that the lines stay away from each other so they do not run into each other when catching the ball or when returning the ball to the tub.

- Make sure the lines don't creep up on you. They need to stay back so you have room to hit the ball.

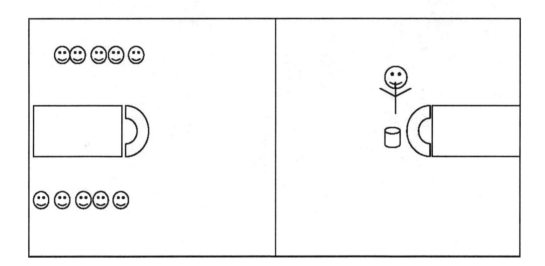

Kick Pin Kick Ball

K-1

Equipment needed: Home plate, hula hoop, pin, gatorskin ball, two poly spots for each game.

We play two games at the same time, one on each half of the gym. Divide the class into teams of four to six players. The fielding team will have one pitcher, standing on a poly spot, a catcher, standing in a hula hoop; and the rest are fielders spread out behind the pitcher. The pitcher rolls the ball to the kicker standing behind home plate. After kicking the ball, the kicker runs to the pin, sitting on a poly spot, 20 to 30 feet away. The kicker kicks the pin down and runs back to home plate. The fielders try to catch the ball and throw it to the catcher. If the catcher has the ball and is standing inside the hoop before the runner gets home, the runner is out. If the runner gets home before the catcher has the ball in the hoop, the runner is safe. We also call the kicker out if the ball is caught in the air, even if it bounces off the wall or ceiling. A ball kicked on the other side of the court is a foul ball. The fielders rotate after each batter: the pitcher goes to catcher, the catcher goes to the outfield, and the outfielders move to their right, with the last fielder on the right going to be the new pitcher. Change sides after everyone on one team kicks. We play games for five to seven minutes and then switch and play a new team.

You can wear pinnies to help identify teams.

Kick pin kickball

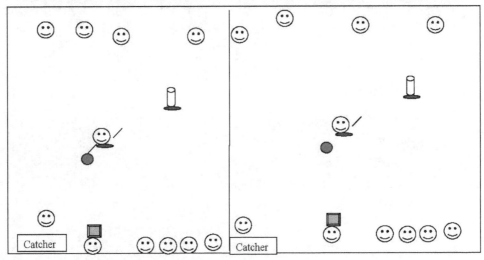

Mat Ball

3rd – 5th

PITCHING

- The Ball (I use a Nerf soccer ball or 8" gator skin ball) is rolled to the kicker
- The pitcher can fake the pitch.
- I have the teams pitch in the same order that they bat.

RUNNERS

- After kicking the ball they run counter clockwise: first base, second base, third base.
- Once the runner is on base they do not have to run.
- There can be more than one runner on a base.
- Runners taking both feet off the base **must** run to the next base, even on a fly ball.
- The runners can steal bases but cannot advance on a foul ball, or on a pitch that is not kicked.

Scoring

- Running all the way around twice. They do not run home. The runner should finish on the same base they started on, first base.
- Five runs per inning limit.

Outs

- A ball caught in the air or off the ceiling in the air is an out.
- A ball that hits the wall and is caught in the air is **not** an out.
- Force outs – player with the ball touches the base the runner is advancing to before the runner gets there.
- **No** throwing at the runners or tagging the runners.

Defense

- The number on the pinnie determines where the players go on defense (<u>see drawing</u>).
- Number one is the first pitcher. The defense rotates after each inning (see drawing).
- The defenders are playing an area.

Other

- I use numbered pennies for both teams.
- **Remind the runners often to watch where they are running.**
- I usually pick the teams.
- Automatic double – any ball that lands behind a table, chairs, or whatever you might have in your gym. My gym is also the lunch room.
- Fair ball – Any ball kicked past the free throw line or designated line.
- Kicking team will kick in the order of their numbers. Number one will kick first.

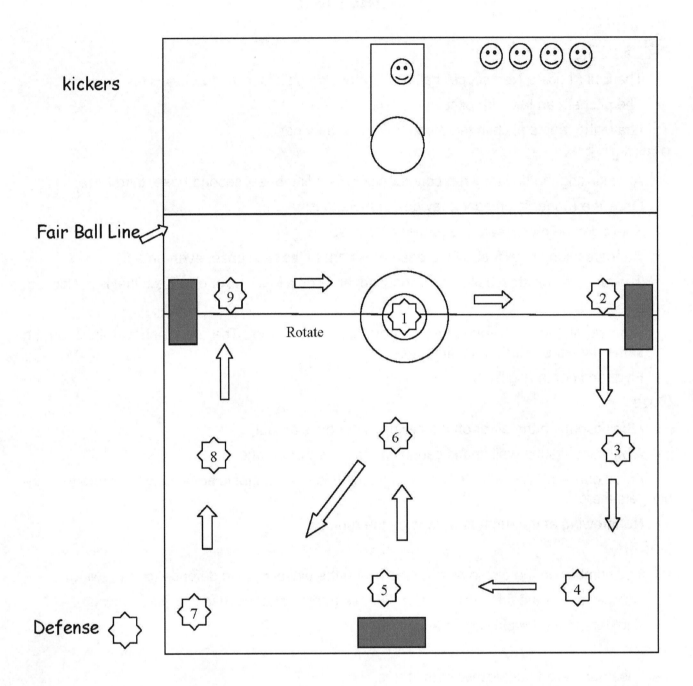

kickers

Fair Ball Line

Rotate

9

1

2

8

6

3

7

5

4

Defense

94

Three-Cone Kickball

1st-3rd

Equipment needed: Three cones (18") for each game, one hula hoop, pin, gatorskin ball for each game (6 ¼" or 7") and floor tape.

Divide the class into teams of four to six people. Use the cones as bases, set about 20 feet apart. I tape an area for home (square). One team will kick and the other is on defense. Play two or three games at the same time. The first person on the kicking team kicks the rolled ball. They run and touch the 1st base cone, 2nd base cone, 3rd base cone and then home without stopping (counterclockwise). The team in the field (defense) gets the ball to the pitcher, who rolls the ball at the pin standing inside the hula hoop near home base. If the pin is knocked down before the runner touches home, the runner is out. If the runner touches home before the pin is knocked down, the runner is safe. We have a catcher behind the pin to roll the ball back to the pitcher to roll again if they miss the pin. Only the pitcher can roll and knock the pin down. We designate a line in the gym or use tape for the pitcher to stay behind when trying to knock down the pin (about 15 feet away). The defense rotates after each person kicks. Each member of the kicking team will kick before the teams trade places.

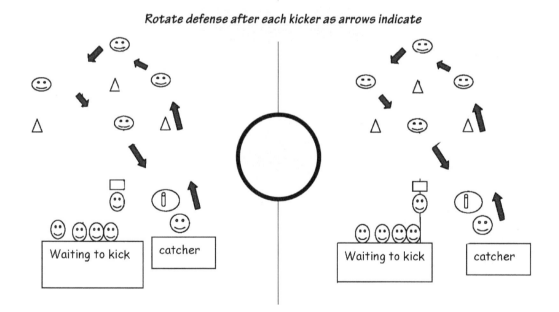

Rotate defense after each kicker as arrows indicate

3-cone kickball

Three Spot Kickball

K-2nd

Equipment needed: Three poly spots, one playground ball or nerf soccer ball or gator skin ball (you determine the size) for each team of three or four people

Divide the class into teams of three or four people. There can be five on a team.

If there are five, there will be two people on deck waiting to kick.

One person is the kicker, one the pitcher, one the outfielder, and one person on deck waiting to kick. The pitcher will roll the ball, nice and easy, and the kicker kicks the ball. The outfielder will retrieve the ball (wherever it goes). The pitcher does not retrieve the ball. Once the outfielder has the ball, the players rotate. The kicker is the outfielder, the outfielder is the pitcher, the pitcher is on-deck and the on deck player is now the kicker.

- The pitcher needs to roll the ball so it can be kicked.
- If the kicker misses the ball, have the pitcher roll the ball again.
- All players need to watch out for other outfielders retrieving their ball and watch out for the ball being kicked by the other teams.
- Have a different color ball for each team if possible.
- Have poly spots the same color as the ball being kicked if possible.
- Rotate teams to a different spot to kick, move down one spot, either way, every four to five minutes.
- If there are four people in a group, the on-deck kicker should not stand right behind the person kicking. They need to give the kicker room to move.

3 spot kick ball

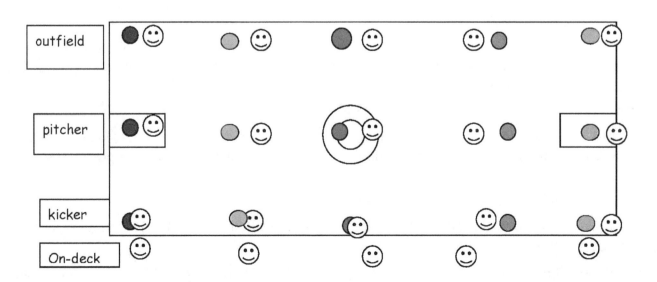

Dribble Rings

2nd – 5th

Equipment needed: 20 to 30 deck tennis rings with a number written on them, one basketball for each ring. There should be at least one ring and one basketball for each student in class.

Place basketballs on deck tennis rings around the gym. Each ring should have a number written on it from 5 to 15. The number tells them how many times to dribble the basketball.

The activity starts with each student standing over a basketball that is resting on a deck tennis ring. On your command, they pick up the basketball and dribble it the number that is on the ring. They put the ball back on the ring and move to another basketball and dribble it the number on that ring. Do this for about two minutes.

Next have the students pick up one ball and the ring it was sitting on. When the music starts, or on your command, students dribble around the gym, holding the ring in their left hand, and dribbling with their right hand for one minute 30 seconds or two minutes. When the music stops, or on your command, they will stop, put the basketball on the ring, walk to another basketball, wait for the music to start, pick up that ball and ring, and dribble with left hand, holding the ring with their right hand. When the music stops, they put the ball on the ring, walk to another basketball and ring. When the music starts, they pick up that ball and ring dribble two or three times with the right hand, then switch the basketball to the left hand and the ring to the right hand.

Partner Activities:

Partners will have one ring and two basketballs.

Round 1: When the music starts the partners will hold the ring with their inside hand and dribble the basketball with their outside hand.

Round 2: Partners switch sides. When the music starts they will dribble again, this time using the other hand.

Round 3: Partners will need one ring and one basketball. Holding the ring with their inside hand, they will dribble two or three times and bounce it to their partner. They dribble two or three times, bounce it to their partner. This continues until the round is over and they switch sides.

Round 4: Switch sides: Holding the ring with their inside hand, they will dribble two or three times and bounce it to their partner. They dribble two or three times, bounce it to their partner.

Tips:

• They stay together while they are dribbling around the gym. If one partner loses control of their basketball they should let go of the ring and get the basketball and go back to their partner.

• Each round will last around two minutes.

• Remind them to watch out for the extra rings and basketballs on the floor as well as other people in the class

• Remind them to stay under control, taking their time to push the basketball using their fingertips and pads of their hands.

Dribble Rings

Pivot Tag

Equipment needed: A basketball for each student, three or four pinnies for the taggers to wear.

Pivot Tag is a tag game we use during our basketball unit. Everyone has a basketball to dribble and three or four people are "IT". As the students dribble around the gym, they are trying not to be tagged by the players that are "IT". When a player has been tagged, that student must hold the basketball with both hands and use a pivot step three times to re-enter the game.

Other Rules

- Players are not allowed to reach across the front of another player to tag.
- If a player loses control of the basketball, double dribbles, or stops dribbling, that is like being tagged, three pivot steps to re-enter.
- Players may not tag the same person twice in the same game until they have tagged all the other players.
- Games last about two minutes.
- You can have more than four people be "IT".
- Players that are "IT" wear a pinnie.

This is not a game of speed. The players must dribble with their head up, dodge and change direction quickly, and have good ball control, using their fingers and the pads of their hands.

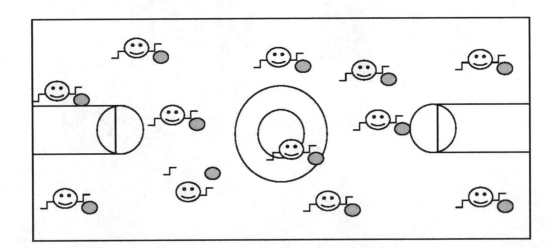

Pivot Tag

Pivot Tag

Tagged players pivoting

Ring Passing

1st - 5th

Equipment needed: Enough basketballs and deck tennis rings for at least half of the class.

Each ring has a number on it ranging from two to ten. Have the rings spread out on the gym floor with a basketball on each ring.

Have the students get a partner. If there is an odd number, there can be a group of three. Demonstrate the chest pass. Then have the partners go to a basketball to perform the chest pass. When they go to a basketball and pick it up, the partners stand on each side of the ring, about three to five feet from the ring. They will chest pass the basketball back and forth the number on the ring. They will be passing over the ring between them. When they finish, they put the basketball back on the ring and go to another basketball. They will start and stop on your command. We do the chest pass, bounce pass, overhead pass. We do the push pass and behind-the-back with older students.

Ring Passing

- Make a good pass to your partner, not too hard or fast, something they can catch.
- Put the ball back on the ring before you move to another.

Disco Bowling

4th – 5th

Equipment needed: Bowling sets, Mirror ball and lights, Disco Music

Our music teacher, Mr. Nichol, is also a DJ, so he has access to many different lighting effects, and sound equipment. He sets the gym up with the lighting and sound, and I set up the bowling lanes. We have four lanes set up in our small gym. We have three to six people at each lane. We keep score on bowling sheets. The first person bowls and the next person to bowl keeps score. The other bowler(s) are down by the pins to set them up and to roll the ball back after the first roll and to carry the ball back to the next bowler after the second roll.

The spotlights are shining down on the pins. I have spots painted on the floor for the pins. We bowl end to end, not side to side.

Bowling Spots

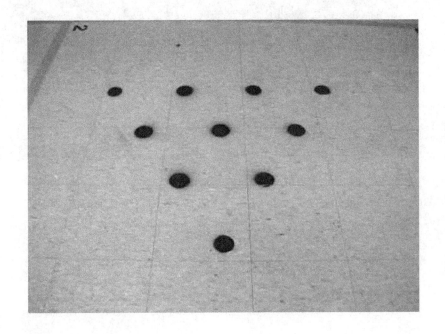

Disco Bowling

Hula Hoop Bowling

Equipment needed: Three poly-spots, one hula hoop, and one ball to roll for each group of three students.

K-1

This is a lead-up activity we use for bowling. Split the class into groups of three. Each group will have one bowler, one hoop holder, and one bowling ball retriever in each group. The bowler gets two tries to roll the ball through the hula hoop. The hoop holder stands to the side of the hoop when holding it. The hoop should be sitting on the poly spot on the floor and is not to be moved when bowling. The retriever rolls the ball back to the bowler, not through the hoop. After two rolls, the bowler becomes the hoop holder, the hoop holder is the retriever, and the retriever becomes the bowler.

- You determine the distance they bowl from; we start about 15 to 20 feet away from the hoop.

- We use the 7" gatorskin ball; you can use another ball to bowl with.

- If the ball is rolled through the hoop on the first roll, the bowler still gets the second roll.

- You can use poly-spots to mark where the bowler should start from

- If you have four people in a group the fourth person can be waiting to bowl. The rotation would be bowler to holder, holder to retriever, retriever to waiting, waiting to bowler.

Hula Hoop Bowling

Pocket Bowling

K – 2nd

Equipment needed: A bowling ball and three bowling pins for each group, and floor tape.

This is an activity I use with K – 2 to teach them about the bowling pocket. In pocket bowling only three pins are set up: the head pin, the number two pin, and the number three pin. The pins are set on tape placed on the floor using the bowling pin stencil. Each bowler is given two attempts to knock down the three pins.

I set up four bowling alleys with three to five people at each alley. Four people works best for us. We have one bowler, one waiting and two people at the other end to set the pins up. When the bowler's turn is over they go to the other end to help set up pins, and one person comes up to wait their turn. I set the pins up about 20 feet away from the bowler. You can determine the distance for your students.

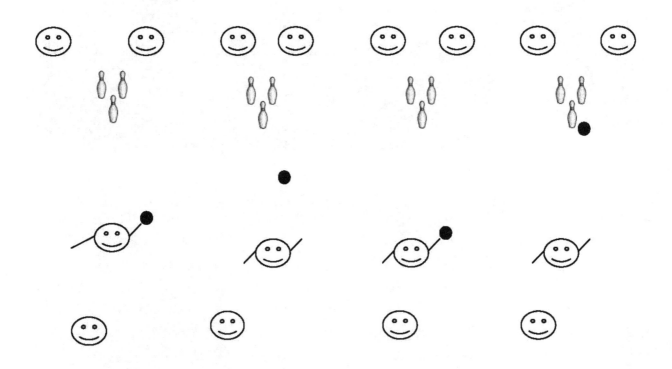

Pocket Bowling

Poly Spot Bean Bag Bowling

K-2

Equipment needed: 20 – 30 poly spots, enough bean bags to have one for each person

Spread the poly spots out around the gym. Have the students get a partner. Give each pair one bean bag. When the music starts, or on your command, the students walk around the gym (any direction). Partners do not walk together. When the music stops, or on your command, each person finds a poly spot to stand on. The partner with the bean bag will find their partner and (bowl) slide the bean bag to their partner, who keeps it. Start the music and repeat the activity. After a few minutes give the other partner a bean bag so that both partners have a bean bag. Now, when the music stops, partners will find a poly spot and they will both (bowl) slide their bean bag at the same time to their partner.

You can have the students skip, gallop, crab walk, etc. instead of walk when the music is playing.

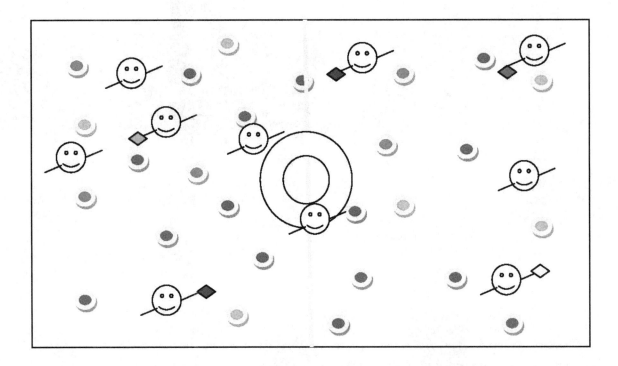

Spilled Milk Bowling

K-2

Equipment needed: 16 poly spots and ½ gallon milk containers (cardboard, not plastic) and, enough bean bags for each student in the class.

This is a variation of the game Bean Bag Bowling submitted to Great Activities by Sandy Thies.

Divide the class into two teams. Each team will have one side of the gym. Set up eight ½ gallon cardboard milk containers on poly spots on each side of the gym. We set them up around the top of the key on each side. Each player should have a bean bag to slide. The object of the game is to slide the bean bag (like they are bowling) and spill the other team's milk (knock down the milk cartons). The first team to knock down the other team's milk cartons wins the game. They cannot pass half court. We do not allow them to protect the milk cartons. Have the teams trade sides after the second game.

Tips

- Change the distance of the milk cartons if the game is too easy or too hard
- You can set a time limit for each game.
- Change the teams, play boys against girls, or short sleeves against long sleeves, etc.
- I usually throw out extra bean bags for the players to slide.
- White foam pins (glasses of milk) could be substituted for the milk cartons.

Spilled Milk Bowling

Spilled Milk Bowling

Spilled Milk Bowling

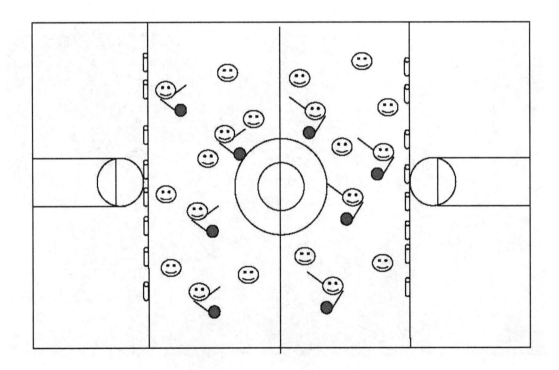

Tic-Tac-Toe Pin Bowling

K-3

Equipment needed: One bowling ball for each game, three poly spots for each game, one pin for each game, a tic-tac-toe board taped to the floor by each game, and ten bean bags for each game, five of one color and five of another color.

Have students partner up and divide the class into groups of four. Each group of four will be playing their own game. The teams of two will stand behind a poly spot equal distance away from a pin. The pin is placed on a poly spot, in the middle of the gym between the two teams. One team will have the bowling ball. The first player will roll the ball to knock down the pin. If they miss, they the go to the end of their line and then the other team will roll. If the pin is knocked down, the bowler that knocked the pin down will place a bean bag on the tic-tac-toe board and set up the pin. Then the other team will roll. Hit or miss, teams and players alternate bowling the ball at the pin. The object of the game is to roll the bowling ball and knock the pin down so they can place a bean bag on the tic-tac-toe board. Teams are trying to get three bean bags in a row on the board and win the game.

Play four or five minutes and have the teams rotate to play another team.

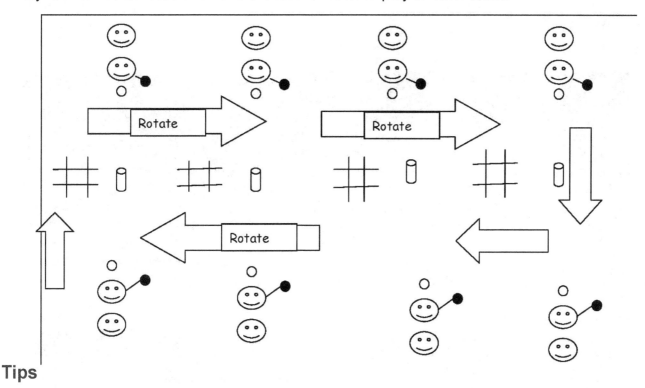

Tips

- You may have three on a team or a team of one if needed
- You can use rings, rubber animals, wooden donuts, etc. instead of bean bags for the tic-tac-toe board.
- You can use foam pins instead of bowling pins, and a gator or playground ball instead of the rubber bowling ball.
- We rotate every team clockwise when we start a new game so they bowl against a new team.

Tic -Tac-Toe Pin Bowling

Tic-Tac-Toe Pin Bowling

Castle Building Pin Soccer

K-3

Equipment needed: Twelve foam pins, rag ball soccer balls, one for each player.

Divide the class into two teams. One team is on each side of the gym. Pick one player from each team to be the castle builder. The castle builder will be on the opposite side of the gym of their team. Set up six pins on each side of the gym. Each team must stay on their side of the gym. To start the game, give each player a rag ball soccer ball. On your signal to start, the players from each team will kick the soccer balls and try to knock down the other team's pins. When a pin is knocked down, the castle builder will pick the pin up to build their castle.

- If a player knocks down a pin on their side, they will stand it back up on the line.
- Players can go into the middle to get a soccer ball, but must dribble it back behind the line before kicking it.
- Players cannot protect their pins.
- I put a piece of gym floor tape on the floor under the pin so they can be reset easily.
- You can use fewer soccer balls.

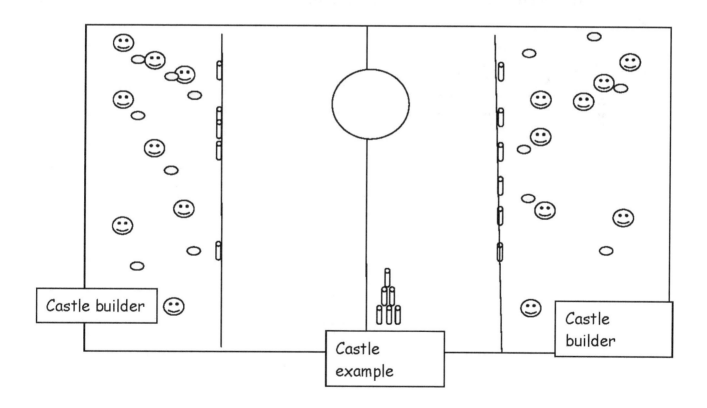

Dribble, Pass and Trap Soccer

Equipment needed: 30 to 50 poly spots (four or five different colors), 1 rag ball soccer ball for half of your students.

Have the students partner up. You can have groups of three. To start the activity, have one partner get a soccer ball and stand on a green spot. I have the other partner stand on a red spot. When the music plays, or on your command, the partner with the soccer ball dribbles it around the gym while the other partner walks around the gym. They can walk in any direction. Stop the music, or blow the whistle, and call out a color for the partner dribbling to trap the ball on. The other partner goes to one of the red spots. The partners locate each other and the soccer ball is passed to the partner on the red spot, who traps the ball with their foot. When the music starts the partners switch roles.

Reminders:

- All students will be traveling in different directions, so they need to watch where they are going (heads up).
- Keep the ball on the ground when passing. Use the inside or outside of the foot.
- Trap the ball with their feet.
- The partner without the ball always goes to a red spot to receive a pass when the music stops.

Dribble, Pass, and Trap Soccer

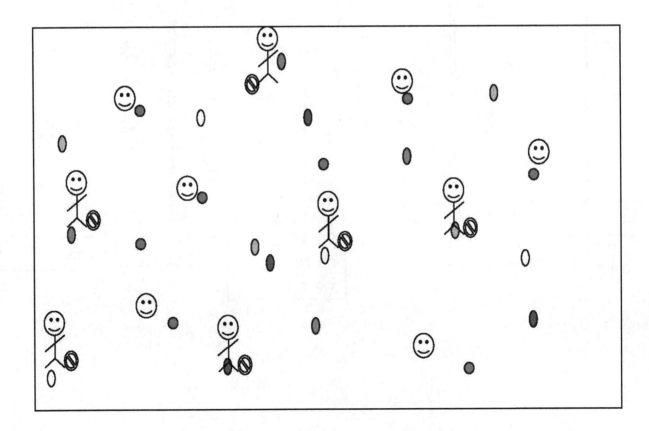

116

Soccer Dribble and Exercise

1ˢᵗ – 3rd

Equipment needed: One soccer ball for each set of partners.

Round 1: Sit and dribble

One partner sits cross legged inside the box area. The people in the box should be at least three feet away from each other and two or three feet away from the sides of the box. The other partner dribbles around the people sitting in the box. They should try to dribble around all the people sitting without hitting them or going outside the box. After 45 seconds or a minute (you set the time), have the partner dribble to the sitting partner and trade places. Each partner should have at least two turns at dribbling.

Round 2: Stand and dribble

One partner stands inside the box area. The people in the box should be at least three feet away from each other and two or three feet away from the sides of the box. The other partner dribbles around the people standing in the box. They should try to dribble around all the people standing without hitting them or going outside the box. After 45 seconds or a minute (you set the time) have the partner dribble to the standing partner and trade places. Each partner should have at least two turns at dribbling.

Round 3 : Tunnel dribbling (standing with feet apart)

   One partner stands with their feet apart inside the box area. The people in the box should be at least three feet away from each other and two or three feet away from the sides of the box. The other partner dribbles through the legs of the people standing in the box. They should try to dribble through all the people standing without hitting them or going outside the box. After 45 seconds or a minute (you set the time), have the partner dribble to the standing partner and trade places. Each partner should have at least two turns at dribbling.

Round 4: Crab Dribbling

   Students are sitting with their feet on the floor and their hands behind them. When a person dribbling a soccer ball comes near, the partner sitting should push up to the crab position so the people dribbling can dribble the soccer ball under them to the other side. The person dribbling should watch out for the fingers of the partner in the crab position. The person inside can relax and sit if there is not a person around to dribble under them. Two or three turns for each partner.

Round 5: Push-up dribbling

Students inside the box are lying on their stomach. When a person dribbling a soccer ball comes close to them, the partner lying down should raise up in the push-up position so the people dribbling can dribble the soccer ball under them to the other side. Two or three turns for each partner.

Round 6: Open /Closed

One partner stands inside the box area. The people in the box should be at least three feet away from each other and two or three feet away from the sides of the box. When you call "closed", one partner dribbles around the people standing in the box without hitting them or going outside the box. When you call "open", they should try to dribble through the legs of the people standing in the box without hitting them or going outside the box. After 45 seconds or a minute (you set the time), have the partner dribble to the standing partner and trade places. Each partner should have at least two turns at dribbling.

OPEN

CLOSED

Foxtail Volleyball

4ᵗʰ – 5th

Equipment needed: One volleyball net, one foxtail

Divide the class into two teams of six to twelve people.

This game is played like a game of volleyball except we throw a foxtail instead of using a volleyball.

The game starts by having the back right person on one team serving, throwing the foxtail over the net. The other team tries to catch the foxtail and throw it back over the net. If the foxtail hits the ground, inbounds, the person who missed it is out and goes to the sideline. If the foxtail is thrown out of bounds, the thrower is out and goes to the sideline. After the third throw both teams rotate. The foxtail can be thrown during rotation.

A team can use three throws to get the foxtail over the net. The foxtail can be thrown to a teammate . The player with the foxtail cannot take more than two steps before throwing it. The foxtail can be played off of the net, except on the serve.

A player that is out may return to their position when a player on the other team is put out of the game.

If a team has three players out at the same time, the other team wins and a new game is started.

Games last no longer than three minutes. If no team has won in three minutes, start a new game.

Foxtail Volleyball

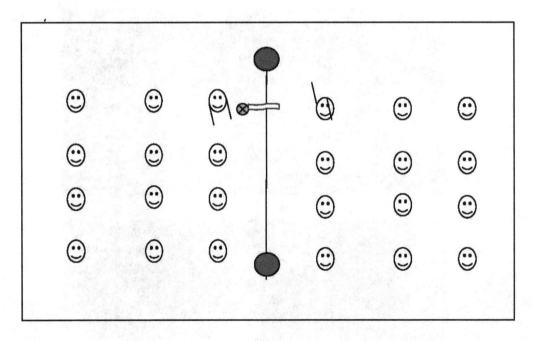

I Got Caught

K-2

Equipment Needed: Volleyball net and yarn balls.

Have the class partner up. Divide the class into two teams. Place one partner on each side of the net. There should be one yarn ball for every two people. The players throw the yarn balls back and forth over the net. If a ball thrown over the net is caught in the air by a person on the other team, the person who threw the ball says "I got caught" and has to go over to the other team. Games will last two minutes. The side with the most players at the end of a game wins.

Other:

- We talk about the release point when throwing over the net.
- We talk about the thrower tracking the ball after it is thrown to see if it hits the ground or if it is caught by someone on the other team.
- We talk about catching with the hands and not the body. A ball above the waist, fingers up, a ball below the waist, fingers down.

Safety:

- I tell them to stay in an area. We define the size of that area before we start the game. They cannot run over others to get to a ball. They can always move to another area during a game.
- No diving or sliding to catch a ball.
- I also play "I Got Caught" using soft volleyballs with the 3rd grade. The students serve the volleyball over the net instead of throwing the ball.

Service Help Volleyball

4th – 5th

Equipment needed: Volleyball, Volleyball net.

   We play a modified game of Volleyball with our fourth and fifth grade students. Most of the rules of Volleyball apply except for the rules of serving. Players will try to serve the ball over the net. If the volleyball is not going to make it over the net it can be caught by a teammate who can then serve the ball over. Many students can serve the volleyball over the net but for the players that struggle this modification helps them feel more confident and they enjoy playing the game more. It also helps keep everyone involved and more interested in the game because the ball may be coming to them.   We also have a rule that no one can have more than three consecutive serves. This rule prevents one player from dominating a game when serving.

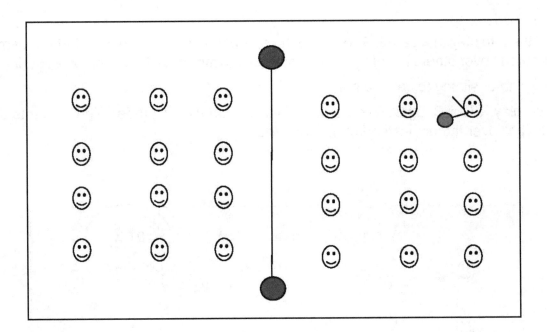

Service Stations Volleyball

1st – 3rd

Equipment needed: 15 to 20 soft volleyballs, two beach balls, two or three 7 inch and four or five 8 inch eurosoft or gatorskin balls, two 4 x 8 mats, one net (badminton net), two poles or standards to hold the net.

The activity: We do this activity after I have shown them how to serve. We are working on the underhand serve. There are five service stations in the gym. Split the class into five groups of four people. There can be more people or less people in a group. The third grade will also work on the bump to reinforce what they have learned.

1. Wall serve:

Students stand about 20 feet away from the wall and serve toward the wall, get the rebound and serve again. Watch out for the other volleyballs and servers. The third grade students may work on the overhand or sidearm serve.

2. Net serving:

Students will have a partner at this station. Have the net four or five feet high and have one partner on each side of the net. They will serve a eurosoft or gatorskin ball back and forth over the net. They should catch the ball in the air when it comes over the net, if they can. I have the third grade students try to bump the ball when it is served over the net.

3. Make a basket:

At this station we use an eight inch eurofoam or gatorskin ball. The students, standing about 10 to 15 feet from the basketball goal, are trying to serve the ball (underhand serve) into the basket. The third grade students may also try to bump the ball into the basket. The basket is at a regulation 10 feet.

4. Box Serve:

Two mats are standing up about 20 feet away from the serving line to make a box. Students stand behind the line and try to serve the ball into the box. They serve the same ball until they make it into the box, then get another ball to serve.

5. Beach Ball Serve:

Students partner up at this station and serve the beach ball back and forth to each other. I have the third grade students serve and bump the beach ball.

Fish and Frogs

K-2

Equipment needed: six to twelve small rubber fish and frogs, six large frogs, six large rubber fish. Rocket launcher boards (two or more), one 4 x 8 mat, 1 small pool, toss nets, playground balls, one 16" scooter, four or more fishing poles (string tied to wooden dowels with a magnet glued to the end of the string), 40 to 50 laminated fish pictures, with a large paper clip attached, four chairs, eight hula hoops. Seven cones and six numbers (1,2,3,4,5,6) to put on six of the cones.

The Activity: Divide the class into groups of four. You can have groups of three or five if needed. Place each group at a station to start the activity. A cone is placed at each station with a number on it. Groups will rotate by number, 1 to 2, 2 to 3, etc.

Station 1:

Gone fishing- Students will sit in a chair and catch fish from their pond using their fishing pole. They will drop the magnet onto the paper clip, lift the fish out and shake it off next to the hoop (pond). When all the fish are caught, the student will re-stock the pond by putting the fish back in the hoop. Use ten to twelve fish at each pond.

Gone Fishing

Station 2:

Jumping Catfish- Students will place a small rubber fish on a rocket launcher, sitting on a 4 x 8 mat, and try to make it land in the pond (small pool) located just behind the mat. The rocket launcher should hang off the end of the mat just a little. Use two launchers and have students take turns.

Station 3:

Frog water Taxi- The first student in line will lay on a 16" scooter on their stomach, and the next student in line will lay a large rubber frog on the back of the student on the scooter. The student will travel on the scooter, using their hands and feet, down around the cone and back. When they return, the next student will go. Place the cone about ten feet away.

Station 4:

Lily Pad Toss- Students stand about ten feet away from four to six hula hoops (lily pads) lying on the floor. They will toss large rubber frogs, trying to make them land in the hoops (on the lily pad). I also used the plastic circle of a loloball. You can use different size hoops and small frogs, one frog for each student.

Station 5:

Fish Net Toss- Students will toss rubber fish and frogs with a toss net and try to catch them. You can have a toss net for each set of partners or you can have three or four people use the same net. They can toss one or more at a time.

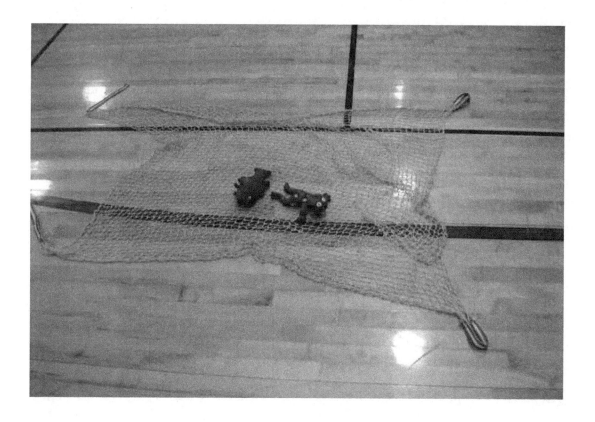

Station 6:

Frog Jumping- Students will use an 8 ½" playground ball and a small rubber frog. They will place the frog on top of the ball. When the students drop the ball the frog will bounce (jump) off, going different heights and directions. The ball has to be dropped, not tossed up or thrown down.

Tips:

- I like to use music during the activity. I stop the music and rotate every three minutes.

- Having the rocket launcher (stomper) hang off the end of the mat just a couple of inches will help launch the frog higher and farther. The mat will also help protect the floor and keep the noise down. I do not give the students running room at this station.

- The toss nets are very slick when left on our wood floor. Students should be careful when going to and leaving this station.

- Having the student's fish in their own pond and not in one big pond keeps the strings from being tangled. They don't fight over the fish.

Halloween Station Activities

K-2

Equipment needed at each station:

1. Four stompers, foam bats, pumpkin balls, ghost, and two mats (optional)
2. Eight bean bags, five to seven laminated pumpkins.
3. Four foam pins, four laminated ghost, and four gatorskin balls.
4. Four scoops, four spider balls.
5. Two ghost and two ropes, one basketball goal to tie the ghost on.
6. Four or five mats and 100 to 200 wooden donuts.
7. Halloween Music.

Split the students up into groups of two to four people.

Station 1

Flying bats, ghost and pumpkins. The students can place one or more items on their stomper. I do not give them a lot of room to run and jump on the board and I put a mat under the boards to protect the floor and help with the noise. They will try and catch what they send flying in the air.

Stompers

Station 2

Smashing Pumpkins: Students stand about ten feet away from the laminated pumpkins that are taped to the wall. They will throw the bean bags at the pumpkins. They should not throw if someone is in front of them picking up their bean bags.

Station 3

Ghost Bowling: Students will stand about ten feet away from four pins, with a laminated ghost attached to the pin. The pins are standing up. Students will roll a gator skin ball at the ghost pins to knock them down. The person knocking the pin down will stand it back up.

Ghost Bowling

Station 4

Catching Spiders: Students will toss spiders in the air and catch them with a scoop. They can catch them in the air or let them bounce and then catch the spider.

Catching Spiders

Station 5

Ghost Buster: Two ghosts are tied to a basketball goal. Students standing about ten feet away will throw a yarn ball and try to hit (bust) a ghost. Try tying them up with fishing line to make the ghosts look they are floating in the air.

Ghost Busters

Station 6

Dracula's Castle: Students will use wooden donuts to build Dracula's castle.

Dracula's Castle

(wooden donuts-core plugs, bungs are used at the ends of large rolls of paper)

Tips:

- I rotate every three minutes.
- We use pairs of different colored bean bags to throw at the pumpkins.
- They need to be careful not to throw the donuts or knock them down on another person. They also need to keep the donuts on the mat because they are very slick if they are stepped on when they are on the floor.
- I use rubber bands to hold the bats and ghost on the foam pins.
- I put tape on the floor to set the ghost pins on.
- I use cotton jump ropes to tie the ghost on the basketball goal.

Scooterville

K-1

Equipment Needed: cones, Seven 16" scooters (two scooters will be connected), one scoop, ten white yarn balls, four hula hoops, ten bean bags, one mail box, four to six poles, two or three jump ropes, a roll of streamers (white), three 4 x 8 folded mats.

Students are traveling around town on their scooters.

The Stations:
Station 1. Going for Ice Cream:

Students sit on the scooter with a scoop on their lap. They travel forward to a hoop filled with white 3" yarn balls (ice cream). They get one scoop of ice cream, one yarn ball in the hoop, and travel back to the line putting the yarn ball in the hoop next to the line and giving the scoop and the scooter to the next person in line. Everyone goes until the yarn balls have all been scooped up. The second round start from the other end and players get two scoops of ice cream (one scoop, two yarn balls).

Station 2. Deliver the Mail:

Students take one alphabet bean bag from the hula hoop and sit on a scooter carrying the bean bag. They travel forward to the mail box, open it and put the letter inside. If all the letters have been delivered, then have the students pick up the mail by taking out one bean bag at a time and returning it to the hula hoop. Another box can be used instead of a mailbox.

Station 3. Car Wash:

Lying on their stomach, students will use their arms and legs to move between and under poles, with streamers hanging down. They travel down and back through the car wash, with the streamers brushing their backs as they go through. Flag football flags could be used instead of streamers.

Car Wash

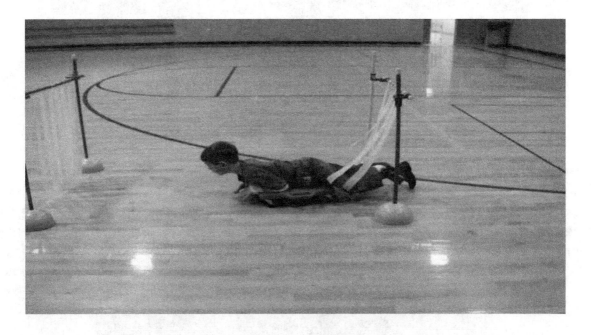

Station 4. Car Pool:

Connect two scooters together. Have two students sitting on the scooters. They will travel down around the cone and back to the line.

Car Pool

Station 5. Paper Boy/Girl:

Students sitting on the scooter with a rolled up newspaper (taped) on their lap will travel down to the cone, stop, and throw the paper on the "porch." The porch is a folded 4 x 8 mat lying on the floor next to the wall. You determine the distance they will throw from. Swimming pool noodles cut to the size of a newspaper can be used to throw if you do not have newspapers.

The newspapers can be in a hula hoop or a milk crate next to the starting cone.

Station 6. Parallel Parking:

Students will sit on a scooter, travel backwards and park between two 4 x 8 folded mats lying on the floor. After parking, they will travel backwards back to the line so the next person can go.

- I have four to six students in a group, and we stay two or three minutes at each station. Class size and time will determine what you do.

138

Chapter 4

Reproducible Handouts & Pictures

Squirrel

Armadillo

Snake

Raccoon

Alligator

Skunk

Bobcat

Baseball Cards

We make baseball cards for the 5th grade class to go along with our unit on baseball/softball. I collected cards as a kid and I remember that the cards would have an interesting or fun fact about the player on the back of the card, so we use that on our cards. The facts do not have to be about baseball. The cards we make are bigger than a baseball card. We put students' pictures in the space above their name. I use their yearbook photos. Students circle the appropriate letter for throwing and batting and write in the fun fact. The cards are put on a bulletin board in the gym.

Baseball Card	Baseball Card
  Name: Mr. Bohannon **Position**: Pitcher **Throws** L ⓡ **Bats** ⓛ R **Fun Fact**: Mr. Bohannon played baseball growing up with Mr. Heim who is the PE teacher at the high school.	Name:_____ Position:_____ Throws L R Bats L R Fun Fact:

Baseball Cards

Baseball Card	Baseball Card
Name :	Name:
Position:	Position:
Throws: L R	Throws: L R
Bats: L R	Bats: L R
Fun Fact:	Fun Fact:

Color Wheel

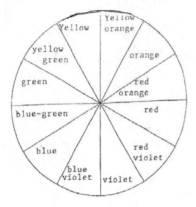

Color Wheel

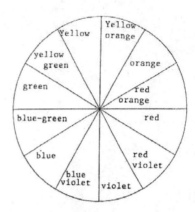

1. Name_____

2. Name_____

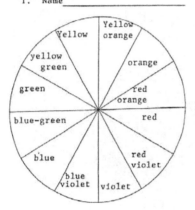

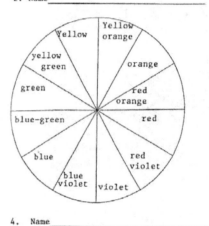

3. Name_____

4. Name_____

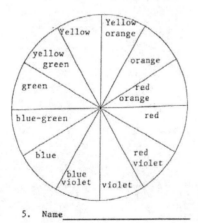

5. Name_____

1. Blue-Violet
2. Blue
3. Blue-Green
4. Green
5. Yellow-Green
6. Yellow
7. Yellow-Orange
8. Orange
9. Red-Orange
10. Red
11. Red-Violet
12. Violet

146

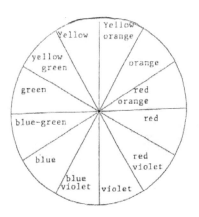

Color Wheel

1. Name_____

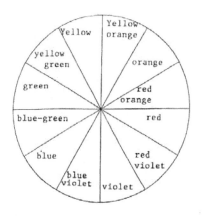

2. Name_____

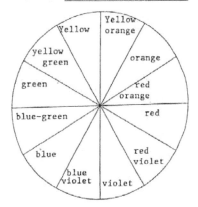

3. Name_____

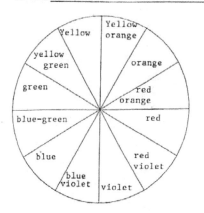

4. Name_____

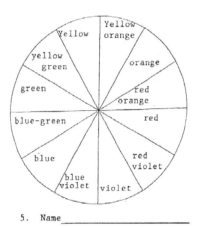

5. Name_____

1.   Red-Violet
2.   Violet
3.   Blue-Violet
4.   Blue
5.   Blue-Green
6.   Green
7.   Yellow-Green
8.   Yellow
9.   Yellow-Orange
10. Orange
11. Red-Orange
12. Red

147

Color Wheel

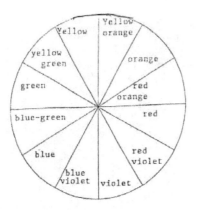

1. Name_____

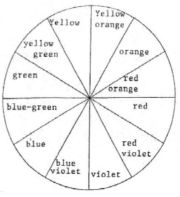

2. Name_____

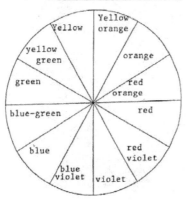

3. Name_____

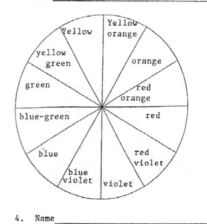

4. Name_____

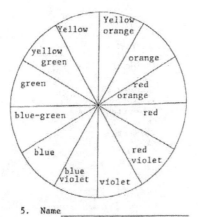

5. Name_____

1. Red-Orange
2. Red
3. Red-Violet
4. Violet
5. Blue-Violet
6. Blue
7. Blue-Green
8. Green
9. Yellow-Green
10. Yellow
11. Yellow-Orange
12. Orange

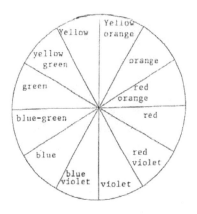

Color Wheel

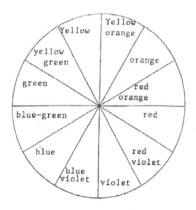

1. Name_____

2. Name_____

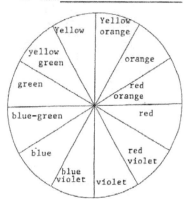

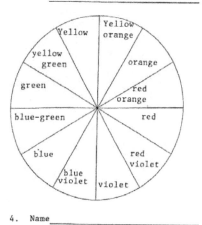

3. Name_____

4. Name_____

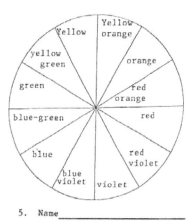

1. Yellow
2. Yellow-Orange
3. Orange
4. Red-Orange
5. Red
6. Red-Violet
7. Violet
8. Blue-Violet
9. Blue
10. Blue-Green
11. Green
12. Yellow-Green

5. Name_____

149

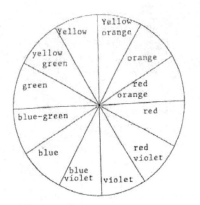

Color Wheel

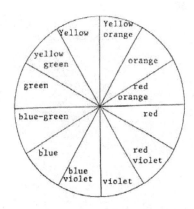

1. Name_____

2. Name_____

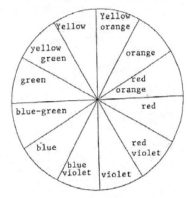

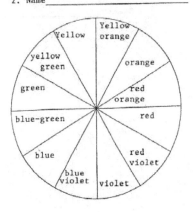

3. Name_____

4. Name_____

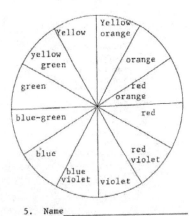

5. Name_____

1. Orange
2. Red-Orange
3. Red
4. Red-Violet
5. Violet
6. Blue-Violet
7. Blue
8. Blue-Green
9. Green
10. Yellow-Green
11. Yellow
12. Yellow-Orange

150

Dice Kicker Number Recognition/Kindergarten

#	BLUE	BLUE	BLUE	BLUE	BLUE	BLUE		RED	RED	RED	RED	RED	RED
#	1	2	3	4	5	6		1	2	3	4	5	6

Write the number the dice lands on in the appropriate column.

Dice Kickers Graphing

#	BLUE	BLUE	BLUE	BLUE	BLUE	BLUE		RED	RED	RED	RED	RED	RED
12													
11													
10													
9													
8													
7													
6													
5													
4													
3													
2													
1													
#	1	2	3	4	5	6		1	2	3	4	5	6

Dice Kickers Math/Addition

	+		=	
	+		=	
	+		=	
	+		=	
	+		=	
	+		=	
	+		=	
	+		=	
	+		=	
	+		=	
	+		=	
	+		=	
	+		=	
	+		=	
	+		=	
	+		=	

	+		=	
	+		=	
	+		=	
	+		=	
	+		=	
	+		=	
	+		=	
	+		=	
	+		=	
	+		=	
	+		=	
	+		=	
	+		=	
	+		=	
	+		=	
	+		=	

Dice Kickers/Subtraction

	-		=			-		=	
	-		=			-		=	
	-		=			-		=	
	-		=			-		=	
	-		=			-		=	
	-		=			-		=	
	-		=			-		=	
	-		=			-		=	
	-		=			-		=	
	-		=			-		=	
	-		=			-		=	
	-		=			-		=	

Dice Kickers/Multiplication

	X		=				X		=	
	X		=				X		=	
	X		=				X		=	
	X		=				X		=	
	X		=				X		=	
	X		=				X		=	
	X		=				X		=	
	X		=				X		=	
	X		=				X		=	
	X		=				X		=	
	X		=				X		=	
	X		=				X		=	
	X		=				X		=	

half
note

Treble Clef

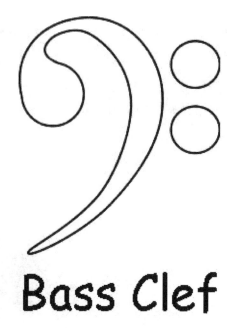

Bass Clef

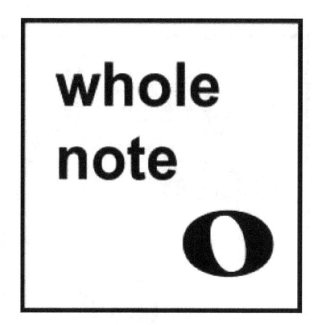

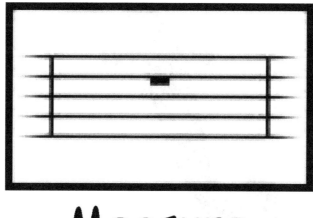

Measure

Crescendo

Percentage Bowling

Name	1		2		3		4		5		6		7		8		9		10		total	
	/10	%	/10	%	/10	%	/10	%	/10	%	/10	%	/10	%	/10	%	/10	%	/10	%	/	%
	/10	%	/10	%	/10	%	/10	%	/10	%	/10	%	/10	%	/10	%	/10	%	/10	%	/	%
	/10	%	/10	%	/10	%	/10	%	/10	%	/10	%	/10	%	/10	%	/10	%	/10	%	/	%
	/10	%	/10	%	/10	%	/10	%	/10	%	/10	%	/10	%	/10	%	/10	%	/10	%	/	%
	/10	%	/10	%	/10	%	/10	%	/10	%	/10	%	/10	%	/10	%	/10	%	/10	%	/	%

Name	1		2		3		4		5		6		7		8		9		10		total	
	/10	%	/10	%	/10	%	/10	%	/10	%	/10	%	/10	%	/10	%	/10	%	/10	%	/	%
	/10	%	/10	%	/10	%	/10	%	/10	%	/10	%	/10	%	/10	%	/10	%	/10	%	/	%
	/10	%	/10	%	/10	%	/10	%	/10	%	/10	%	/10	%	/10	%	/10	%	/10	%	/	%
	/10	%	/10	%	/10	%	/10	%	/10	%	/10	%	/10	%	/10	%	/10	%	/10	%	/	%

Name	1		2		3		4		5		6		7		8		9		10		total	
	/10	%	/10	%	/10	%	/10	%	/10	%	/10	%	/10	%	/10	%	/10	%	/10	%	/	%
	/10	%	/10	%	/10	%	/10	%	/10	%	/10	%	/10	%	/10	%	/10	%	/10	%	/	%
	/10	%	/10	%	/10	%	/10	%	/10	%	/10	%	/10	%	/10	%	/10	%	/10	%	/	%
	/10	%	/10	%	/10	%	/10	%	/10	%	/10	%	/10	%	/10	%	/10	%	/10	%	/	%
	/10	%	/10	%	/10	%	/10	%	/10	%	/10	%	/10	%	/10	%	/10	%	/10	%	/	%

Scavenger Hunt

Item or Activity	Points	Points Earned
10 jumping jacks	5	_____
10 push-ups	5	_____
5 sit-ups	5	_____
10 rope jumps	5	_____
10 hula hoops (waist)	5	_____
Shoot 3 shots inside the lane	5	_____

• Find the following items

Item	Points	Points Earned
A penny	1	_____
A wooden nickel	5	_____
A yellow Alligator	5	_____
$\frac{1}{2}$ a tennis ball	4	_____
A badminton birdie	10	_____
X-Ray	3	_____
Bean bag	2	_____
Dice	6	_____
Total Points page 1		_____

Scavenger Hunt

Item	Points	Points Earned
• Deck tennis ring	1	_____
• Plastic egg	1	_____
• Volleyball	1	_____
• An eraser	2	_____
• A clothes pin	10	_____
• A penny money wrapper	10	_____
• **Special** (in your group points)		
• Anyone wearing glasses	5	_____
• Anyone wearing braces	5	_____
• Anyone wearing a watch	5	_____
• Everyone in your group Is wearing tennis shoes	10	_____
• Everyone in your group Is wearing white socks	10	_____
Total points page 2		_____
Total points page 1 and 2		_____

These pages are a list some of the things we use in our scavenger hunt.

Turkey Hunt

Extras

Deck Tennis Rings

I use deck tennis rings for relay type activities. The first person in line has the ring. They will carry the ring, when they return to the line they will hand the ring to the next person in line so they can go. A person cannot go if they do not have the ring.

Another use for deck tennis rings is to hold equipment. You can put a basketball, volleyball, soccer ball etc. on them so they don't roll away.

Deck Tennis Rings can also be used to keep partners together. If they both have to hold onto the ring they can't get too far apart.

Frisbees

I like to use Frisbees to cover objects up instead of using cones.

I use foam Frisbees for tag games. The people who are "it" use a foam Frisbee to tag instead of using their hands.

Hula Hoops

I use hula hoops for collection areas. Card activities, items collected in matching games, I also use them for pin placement or a restricted area for juggling.

Numbered Pinnies

I use numbered pinnies when playing baseball or kickball type games. The number on the pinnie determines the batting order, the player wearing Number 1 bats first etc., and the pitching order, if the kids are pitching. I sometimes reverse the order and the last number to be the first batter or pitcher. There is no doubt who is up next or who they bat or kick after. I also use the numbers to rotate the players to a new position on defense.

 Mike Bohannon has taught elementary physical education for 25 years. He earned a B.S. in Physical Educa-tion and an M.S. in Education from the University of Kansas. He has had many games published in the Great Activities Newspaper for Elementary and Middle School Physical Education.

CPSIA information can be obtained
at www.ICGtesting.com
Printed in the USA
BVHW011745080719

552852BV00016B/342/P

9 781935 018742